Raising A Business and Babies

A Christian Woman's Guide to Flourishing at Work and at Home.

By Ashley Schubert

CLC Publishing

Published by CLC Publishing, LLC.
Mustang, OK 73064

Printed in the United States of America

All Bible verses borrowed from "The Message Translation".

Book Design by Shannon Whittington
Cover Design by McKenna Marchetti

ISBN: 9781091668539

Non-Fiction/Inspirational

Table of Contents

Hymn to a Good Wife 7

Introduction 9

Y'all Are Crazy 13

Determining Your Why 29

Rising Strong 41

Speaking Life 53

Don't Miss the Magic 67

Losing Isn't Pretty 79

Nobody Said It Was Easy 91

MOMMIN' With Courage 103

Living Authentically 113

From Surviving to Thriving 123

Fearlessly Forward 139

Conclusion 153

Acknowledgements 155

About the Author 157

Proverbs 31

Hymn to a Good Wife

10-31 A good woman is hard to find,
and worth far more than diamonds.
Her husband trusts her without reserve,
and never has reason to regret it.
Never spiteful, she treats him generously
all her life long.
She shops around for the best yarns and
cottons,
and enjoys knitting and sewing.
She's like a trading ship that sails to faraway
places
and brings back exotic surprises.
She's up before dawn, preparing breakfast
for her family and organizing her day.
She looks over a field and buys it,
then, with money she's put aside, plants a
garden.
First thing in the morning, she dresses for work,
rolls up her sleeves, eager to get started.
She senses the worth of her work,
is in no hurry to call it quits for the day.
She's skilled in the crafts of home and hearth,
diligent in homemaking.
She's quick to assist anyone in need,
reaches out to help the poor.
She doesn't worry about her family when it
snows;
their winter clothes are all mended and ready
to wear.
She makes her own clothing,

and dresses in colorful linens and silks.
Her husband is greatly respected
when he deliberates with the city fathers.
She designs gowns and sells them,
brings the sweaters she knits to the dress
shops.
Her clothes are well-made and elegant,
and she always faces tomorrow with a smile.
When she speaks she has something
worthwhile to say
and she always says it kindly.
She keeps an eye on everyone in her
household,
and keeps them all busy and productive.
Her children respect and bless her;
her husband joins in with words of praise:
"Many women have done wonderful things,
but you've outclassed them all!"
Charm can mislead and beauty soon fades.
The woman to be admired and praised
is the woman who lives in the Fear-of-God.
Give her everything she deserves!
Festoon her life with praises!

Introduction

That pesky Proverbs 31 woman. She has it all together, she does it all and she manages to be happy about doing it all. We admire her, we want to be like her and we want to pursue God how she does. This woman was the inspiration for this book. I want to be more like her and I strive for those characteristics every day and pray that God will develop them more and more inside of me.

This book is special because I have lived out all the things that most moms do. I asked friends what their biggest struggles were as a mom and what they would like to improve upon. I discovered that we are all asking ourselves the same questions. Am I being the best mom for my children? Is my business flourishing? Am I failing in multiple areas? Why do I feel so guilty that I like working? I'll address all of these issues and more throughout the pages of this book and give a scripture to contradict women's common thoughts.

Here are the highlights of my path---I got into a business that has a 90% failure rate. That means, I only had a 10% chance of succeeding. My husband and I started businesses simultaneously and have been co-entrepreneurs through all the tests, trials and triumphs. We have 4 children. Society tells us that a mom who has multiple children cannot do both, they must choose- work or family. "You cannot do both well", they say. But I've managed to raise four children, while earning top honors in my industry. Y'all, it can be done!

We need more women who are in the trenches, right now, every day, living the daily life who can share their stories. We need more moms who are living in the messes and the chaos and who can be real and say "me too". We need more Christians who can share their lives authentically. That's why I'm writing this book now, while I'm in the chaos, while I have young children who need me, while I'm busy at work, while everyone needs my attention RIGHT NOW. Because I'm HERE now. I know what's it like not because I've been there but because I am there. I see you. I'm ready to share with you what I know.

I want you to know that it's possible to have a successful business and a happy, flourishing family. It's not only possible- it's totally attainable! It's possible to raise children and build your business simultaneously. You can do this at a high level while maintaining integrity and live a living a life with purpose. I am in this busy season right there with you. I'm constantly changing diapers and cleaning messes, depending on which one of my children has caused the latest shenanigans. I'm locking myself in the bathroom to take a phone call while my kids bang on the door wanting me. I'm sneaking in a shower while my kids come looking for me to open their juice box. I'm learning how to discipline and teach my children in each new season. I'm learning how to structure my team, hire employees, grow my sphere and take the best care of my clients. I do not have it all figured out and each new day, new year and new level presents new challenges.

Looking back, I have been writing this book for almost two years, blogging with bits and pieces of my journey. God was preparing my heart and mind to begin the actual writing of this book in 2019. But he knew it was going to be written long before I did.

I always say the "real estate" is just a tool I use to help other people. It's my platform. I have grown my thriving business into producing a six-figure income, built a quality team and been on several ventures along the way- podcasting, public speaking, leading in various capacities- and having four babies. I've been through plenty of trials, tribulations, relationship failings with friends due to jealousy and misunderstandings. I don't understand it, I can't explain it. But I know that when I decided to write this book, Satan shuddered. I have faced more personal growth opportunities this past year than during any other time of my life.

Through struggles with family, friendships, business issues and determining my self-worth- I have seen it all in the last 12 months. It's as if when I said a big "yes", my world became vulnerable. I have had my integrity and character questioned, lost friendships and faced adversity that have broken me. Despite all of that, I do know this- God uses our struggles for His glory. There isn't one thing that happens is a surprise to Him. Sometimes we must go through difficulties to really grow...and often God allows that to happen. I know this book was supposed to happen, and I know that I am most inspired to write through pain and disappointments.

These pages are filled with words written during difficult days. I hope these words fill you with hope, as you realize that there are certainly valleys ahead. But with God, the valleys are short bumps and the mountain top moments are so much more frequent, consistent and worth it. Now, move forward in faith, knowing there is joy when we seek it.

Each chapter is filled with what women commonly tell themselves, followed by God's truth through scripture. There will also be a practical tip in each chapter which will help in daily life, from home tips to life lessons! I wrote a lot of poetry preparing for this book, and it came to me through some really tough and some really beautiful times, so you'll see my poetry at the end of each chapter. I'm also a quote guru so there will be plenty of my favorite quotes displayed between these pages. I hope you love them as much as I do!

I pray that this book inspires you and helps you strategize as you create your dream life - your family and your business depend on your intentionality right now.

Y'all Are Crazy

What Women Say: "I'm afraid to take risks to create the life I really want."

What God Says: Jesus said to her "Daughter, you took a risk of faith, and now you're healed and whole. Live well, live blessed! Be healed." Mark 5:34

"Are there some days I feel like tearing my hair out and wish I had less laundry, less messes, lower grocery bills and more "me" time? Yes. But this life is not about me. It's about joining hands with Jesus to fulfill whatever tasks He sets before me and to share His love with all He brings my way." Lysa TerkEurst

Practical Tip #1: *Make your bed every day. The end. If I could summarize for you how to jump-start each day, create structure in your life and set your goals, it all starts with this concept. Make it your goal every day to make your bed. When you do this simple practice, which takes all of two minutes, it will make you feel accomplished and ready to conquer the day ahead! Even if the rest of your house isn't clean yet, making your bed first will help you tackle all the tasks that lie ahead!*

The Story

This is the part of the book where I want to tell you about me. I want to tell you how my journey started and the lessons I learned along the way. You may find this part interesting, I hope you do.

I had to believe, when writing this, that you would be affected by hearing my story and that it would light a fire in you. You'll see my life story spread between the pages of this book in many ways, through struggles, successes and the dreams. I want you to see how the common theme of my life is "figuring it out" and "doing it afraid". From one thing to the next, I've had to learn, research, pray, feel God's peace and then GO! I want this chapter to tell you the story of a newly-engaged, broke, jobless, recent college graduate who had no clue what she wanted to do. Of a girl with big dreams but no clear direction. Of a girl who chose to go for it.

Growing Up

I was raised on a ranch overlooking hills and green grass, surrounded by cattle and horses grazing nearby. My parents were both self-employed, loving and caring, and they made their own schedules and plans. My dad was a cattle rancher and my mom owned a salon in the local town for twenty-five years. I fully credit my drive and desire to work hard to my upbringing. My parents showed me what it looked like to be determined and my mom modeled for me what it is to be a strong woman who loves my husband and family most and believe in her dreams. I lived in the country and grew up riding horses, playing outside and spending a lot of time with my family. It was an ideal childhood and for that I am thankful.

I'm reminded of a song I heard and it made me think of how I want my daughter to see me and to think of herself. This is the way my mom raised me, and this is the way I want to raise my daughter as well. Lauren Alaina Song:

When I love, I give it all I got like my mother does.
When I'm scared, I bow my head and pray like my mother does.
When I feel weak and un-pretty, I know I'm beautiful and strong.
Because I see myself like my mother does.

Going to a super small school, I became very well-rounded because I had no choice. Literally, at a small school you must participate in every activity or there won't be enough to fill the team. So, I played basketball, softball, cheerleading and ran track when we had enough who wanted to form a team. I was also Class President and Vice-President, 4-H Club President and the list goes on, you get the idea. Growing up this way made me very competitive and really taught me the value of treating others well. My parents always made it a strong point that we were to "treat the janitor with the same respect as we would the CEO". This has always stuck with me and honestly, it's gotten me a long way in life. When we value people, not taking into account their position or if they can help us, it will come back to us in abundance. It's pretty simple really. Love Jesus and be kind to people, in that order.

College was great. I loved those days so much and looking back, they are still some of the best times of my life. I'm so glad I was able to attend a smaller university where I knew almost everyone on campus. I got to be in all kinds of clubs and events and knew all of my professors by name. The experiences were unforgettable, as the kids today say "epic". I also learned about making mistakes, losing some things I really wanted to win and really just grew up between the ages of 18-22. That time was so instrumental in my transformation from a kid into an adult. I loved that time of my life and it didn't hurt that I met my husband on a blind date during our senior year. This is such a funny story and it could only have been God's timing.

"You really need to meet our friend, Bronson", my friend told me during class one day. I shrugged and kind of blew it off. I had just gotten out of a relationship and wasn't looking for a new one. "Seriously, you guys would be perfect for each other", she went on and on telling me about his great qualities. "He's a senior and he loves the weight room so he is built really well", she went on, "and he works at the meat market in town". What, wait? She wanted me to date a butcher? That was a little weird.

"Okay, one date", I finally gave in, "But it needs to be a group date so it's not so awkward." She hosted a dinner at her house and decided to play board games. I showed up at 7:00 p.m. in my softball cleats and my hair in a ponytail because I had an intramural softball game later that evening. I didn't plan on it really working out with this guy so I figured he may as well see the real me! We met, had dinner with the friends, played board games and then it was time for me to go. "Hey, you want to come watch my softball game?" I asked before I left. He agreed and off we went.

For our second date, he took me out to dinner at a local Italian place. We had a great conversation and I politely told him I only had one hour because I had a Student Government meeting at 7:00, priorities, you know. He said he would drop me off at my meeting after dinner and we had a nice time. I knew another date would follow. That is, if he wasn't too scared away by my over-achiever tendencies to attend evening meetings and my ponytail-wearing, sports playing, sweaty self.

On our third date, he sealed the deal. He cooked me a 22-ounce bone-in ribeye with corn-on-the-cob and baked potatoes at his little apartment. Little did he know, I was raised on a cattle ranch and I loved steak more than anything else on the planet. I polished off that delicious ribeye and he knew at that point that he was going to marry me, so he says.

It took five dates for him to kiss me. We two-stepped to a song that was really popular at that time "You Should Have Seen It In Color" by Jayme Johnson. He did some super fancy moves, twirling me in and out, and kissed me. It was on that date, I knew for sure that he was "the one".

After only 6 months of dating and college graduation, we were ready to make our love story official. So, with an unexpected and surprising proposal, I said "yes"! He proposed to me while I was interning at the local news station. I thought I was doing a mock anchoring session. Little did I know, he had my boss put the words "Ashley, will you marry me?" on the teleprompter screen. I read them out loud and looked around confused. He came out from behind the screen, got down on one knee, I laughed like a crazy woman in shock. "I was wondering if you wouldn't mind marrying me too much?" he asked (We were HUGE Rocky fans back then, and still are, so a Rocky proposal was special!). "Yes, yes, yes" I said as he slipped that ring on my finger. We walked through the last couple months of college and through graduation, hand in hand, and living on love.

Living on Love

After an awesome college experience and a degree, I was engaged and ready to embark on a great life. "You can't live on love" my grandpa said. There we were, two broke recent college grads, with a wedding looming in the near future, we just smiled and nodded. We had gotten engaged after only 6 months of dating and people said "y'all are crazy". This phrase has come to define our whole life. We needed jobs and needed them quickly. The problem was that we really didn't know what we wanted to do. I knew I wanted to work with people, enjoy good hours and be social. I started the job hunt and reached out to former connections that I hoped might land me a post-college job, and I was right!

I took my first job as a Legislative Assistant at the Oklahoma State Capitol. It was fun, I learned a lot and enjoyed the folks I worked with. During this time, I also decided to get my Master's Degree. I didn't need it particularly but I wanted to get more education before we decided to have children and I found a great program. For almost two years, I went to night classes after working my day job, took summer school, scored a sweet study abroad trip to France and worked my tail off to complete that degree. My mom got to go with me on that trip to France and, man-oh-man, we made some great memories. My husband couldn't go with me because 1) We were broke. 2) He couldn't get time off at his new job. It was a wonderful, funny and crazy experience. Have I ever "needed" that degree? No. You don't even need a degree at all in my profession. In that sense, I am over-qualified to do what I do.

I gained so much life experience, skills in writing and speaking and the ability to solve problems through higher education. I'll never regret it. I then took a job at a corporate oil company during the big OKC oil boom and worked there for two years until it was time to start thinking about the next phase of life.

Jump In And Swim

"You should do that. You're good at talking me into things", my husband said, and he had a point. For years, I had learned to "mind-warp", as he called it, when I needed to sell him on something. It didn't take much to convince me. I wanted a career where I could make my own schedule, work with people daily and have no cap on my earnings. I loved the idea of a commission-based career. So, I signed up for my classes and test and knocked them both out in a couple of months. I then signed on with a brokerage and started promoting myself. I literally had to jump in and swim or I was going to sink. During my first year, I sold 20 houses, which kept me very busy and was a big deal for a brand-new agent. I know instantly that I wanted to make it my career and my skill set became my "sweet spot". I was finally getting to do something I loved- helping people, being social, making my own schedule. It was a perfect fit!

Having Babies

I took my real estate exam when I was exactly 40 weeks pregnant. I was determined to pass that silly test before my baby arrived. Praise the Lord, I passed on the second try! When our first baby arrived, a baby girl, I didn't know what I was doing. After a long 66-hour labor, I was pooped. She was a stubborn little thing and still has a mind of her own, which I love. Even though I had no idea how to feed, change or care for a baby, I jumped in and figured it out. She was such a good baby but I found some things to be difficult. Like nursing for instance. No one tells you it's going to feel like a shark is latching onto your breast every time you try for the first week. When you read the books, they say "breastfeeding should not hurt". I call bologna! It does hurt for the first week. It will hurt. Be prepared to curl your toes and clamp down on your lips because it will hurt. And then it gets better. And then it doesn't hurt at all. And then you are pro! But Sister, give yourself some grace and prepare your mind for the beginning stages of having a baby.

When our second little bundle arrived, only 15 short months after the first, we were delighted to have a little boy. To this day, I do not know what I would do without this little man. He is the funniest, sweetest, most kind-hearted human you will ever meet. He is also wild, loud and super fun. He came out in a blaze of glory with us barely having time to arrive at the hospital. My water broke in the middle of the night and we flew down the interstate as fast as we could do get to the hospital. It was literally like a movie. I walked, well I actually I limped into the hospital, pausing for super painful contractions. I had to be at least halfway there, right? Surely, I was dilated to a 5. I laid on the table and, lo and behold, I was already almost a 10! Holy cow! Like, "I just started having labor pains an hour ago", I exclaimed. Well, the nurse smiled "it's time to push". I believe the way babies arrive say a lot about their personalities in life. As stubborn and slow as my first was to arrive, she is still this way now. My second came out 5 days early and in a blaze of glory! He is still fast, fun and hard to contain. The next two would arrive slow, steady and both two weeks late. During this time of going from one baby to two, it was the most challenging for our marriage. Now, you see, my husband was also starting his own business during this time. He worked long hours, was gone each week for training in another state and was consumed with work and the grand opening of his new business. With my business growing and taking more of my time, and two babies (fifteen months apart) that now depended on us, we were definitely feeling the strain. During this time, we definitely had to realize that marriage is about spending quality time together, communicating regularly and really listening to each other. He had to learn that I needed more of his help and time around the house. I had to learn to respect and encourage him, and believe in him most of all. We grew a lot during that year of marriage and for that, I will always be thankful. When parents ask me "What's the hardest transition? Babies 1, 2, 3 or 4? I say, without a doubt, "Going from one to two is the hardest because you must learn how to juggle everything and multi-tasking takes on a whole new meaning.

When you're expecting, you're so focused on that due date. Everyone asks you, from the time you conceive until that very last day "when is the baby arriving?" When that date comes and goes, and there is still no baby it's like a whole new world is opening up and it's constant frustration. Was that a contraction? Nope, just baby burrowing even further down into my pelvis. Did my water just break? Nope again. Just my leaking bladder which cannot take any more weight on it. The mind plays tricks and the more people ask the dreaded question "No baby yet?", the more you want to go into hiding. I knew they meant well, I really did.

But I wanted this baby to come and I was determined that each would come on their own. My doctor assured me the baby was safe and healthy, I had plenty of fluid and baby was thriving. I tried to be patient. I cried and I prayed. Two weeks late, baby boy #3 finally woke me up at 3:00 a.m. and the contractions started. It was a laid-back birth. Nothing crazy, nothing dramatic. Our second baby boy arrived safe and sound and…huge! Weighing in at 9.6 pounds, the doctor shouted "he's a moose". That's what he was, my little moose.

The fourth time around, I thought, "oh yeah, this baby is going to come early". No way he will stay in here past the due date. "We better not travel past 38 weeks" I said. I was just sure this baby would be born on the side of the highway. Wrong again. God had other plans for that sweet munchkin, I went past my due date again. The doctor assured me again that baby was healthy and my body was strong. I continued going to work, going to closings, and smiling for pictures. Deep down, I was a mess. "Why, Lord?", I prayed, "My body is tired, I'm chasing around three kids, Work is crazy, just let me have this baby, Lord. I don't want to be induced, I don't need to be, I have this under control, my body knows what to do." I think God wanted to teach me a lesson. After 42 weeks, my doctor scheduled the inducement. I was mad, frustrated and nervous. I had always gone into labor on my own. The morning of the scheduled inducement, I woke up the Lord speaking into my heart "I have a plan and it's better than yours". I trusted and the day was perfect. Our baby boy, child number four, arrived easily. He was strong and perfect.

I firmly believe God teaches us things through our trials. If things always went perfectly according to plan, we would never learn anything. Mark Batterson writes "We should stop asking God to get us out of difficult circumstances and start asking God what he wants us to get out of difficult circumstances". When we go through trials, when we go through fire, that's when we grow the most.

Just Google It

I've heard that "God moves" often doesn't make sense. I've found that all those times in my life when I felt a direct nudge from the Lord, it usually doesn't make sense. Those are also the times that I have chased and not looked back. Starting a podcast was one of those times. When I had the idea to start my own, I didn't know the first thing about podcasting. I didn't know about equipment, recording, editing, anything really. I just knew that I liked talking to people and I had a platform to share- a platform that I believe women needed to hear. So, I did what every entrepreneur does, I googled it.

And so, as any great endeavor begin, I headed to the Google search bar. I researched what it would take to start my own podcast and within a week bought my equipment and created an account to host my own show. Crazy, right? I've learned that the more risks you take, the more risk-averse you become. Things aren't quite as scary as they seemed when you started taking those baby-step risks way back.

Podcasting has opened up doors and allowed me to meet many people, connect with listeners and develop some communication and interviewing skills that I needed. It has taught me things, and it's empowered me and all the women who listen. When we feel a "God move" coming on we might as well step aside and say "let's do it". You'll be glad you did.

Honey, I Sold the House

I'm just going to say it. I think "forever homes" are boring. I know, I know... I just don't fit the cliché' of buying the forever home for my family and all the hype that it entails. My husband and I like to move when we find the right place and opportunity and we have moved when it didn't make much sense to anyone else.

"Oh hey, babe, I sold our house today", I said to my husband one afternoon on the phone. "Oh really, I didn't know it was for sale", he responded. "Well, I talked to someone who wants to buy it, so I put a price on it. They accepted and we have to find a new place so we can close next month" I said with a smile. This is the life my husband has become accustomed to- bless his heart. But hey, he knew this was his future when he married me.

It's always seemed to work out. After we sold house #2, we found house #3, a charming ranch-style home on acreage with big potential and a magnetic country feel. We fell in love and after a few rounds of negotiating, made it our own. I love this house, I do. But it won't be our forever home. We will always be searching for our next project, our next place to love and our next deal to be had. I can't wait when I can call my hubby again and say "Hey babe, I might have sold our house today".

You Gotta Be A Little Crazy

The thing about being ready is that we are never really ready to do something big. I know I've never been. I wasn't ready to get engaged after only 6 months of dating, wasn't ready to get married at the age of 22, wasn't ready to have my first baby or the ones that followed, wasn't ready to start a brand-new career, wasn't ready to start my husband's new business, wasn't ready to buy our first house or the second or third and so on. You get the point. For all logistical reasons, I wasn't ready. But just because I wasn't ready doesn't mean it wasn't right. It doesn't mean I couldn't do it or wouldn't figure it out. The truth is, God doesn't call us to do hard stuff. He calls us to do impossible stuff. I believe God sets things before us and encourages us to go for them. Through prayers and seeking his guidance, of course. But here is the deal, we actually have to move. We have to take the first step. We have to step out in faith. We have to put in the work. God is not going to drop things into our laps. He is going to equip us, empower us and encourage us, but we must be willing to do the work.

Maybe what God is calling you to do is bigger than you could ever ask, dream or imagine. Here is the key: All you have to do is be willing to say "Yes" to God. I find it miraculous that when I "give it to God" and let Him have control, things happen. Like, things that should have never happened and must have been an act of God, they happen. When I reach the point of surrender, that's when He shows up in the biggest way. In times when you may doubt your calling and your qualification, remember why you started, remember your why. God likes it when there seems to be no way. That's where He makes a way. God doesn't call the qualified, sister. He qualifies the called.

Raising a Business and Babies
By Ashley

My shoulders ache, my mind is tired at the end of
each day.
But I cannot be sad because this is the life for which I
have prayed.

A business and babies, both at once. Both full-time
and both in need of my time.
In both, I feel I can be successful and feel in my
prime.

My greatest attempts at being the perfect mom and
leader, in many times they fail.
But it shows me that without God I am so frail.

There are sometimes when I don't know whether I'm
doing it right or doing it wrong, all that matters is that
my babies and my business know they belong.

My heart longs for days when they can all walk, talk
and play.
But, for now I'll just keep working, discipling and
showing them the way.

Yes, my eyes are tired and my patience on some
days can be short.
But I am happy and whole, of this I can report.

I am raising these babies and this business too.
So, for blessings and provision, I pray for both to
ensue.

Discussion Questions

Write down your story. Make sure you have some things in it that the world may consider "crazy" (wink, wink).

_____

_____

_____

_____

_____

_____

_____

_____

_____

_____

_____

Determining Your Why

What Women Say: "Now that I'm a Mom, I worry that I'm losing myself and my identity."

What God Says: "Use all your skill to put me together; I wait to see your finished product." Psalm 25:21

"It's not enough to have lived. We should be determined to live for something."- Winston S. Churchill

Practical Tip #2: *Place books throughout your home and in places where you live daily. For me, that includes: In my car, in my purse, on my nightstand and beside my chair in the living room. By making books easily accessible, we are more likely to read them. Reading can help us in so many ways and opens our minds to new perspectives and lessons.*

Goal of This Chapter

The goal of this chapter is to help you decide, right now, what you want your life to be based on. Determining your why and setting your life priorities is one of the most important things you will ever do. It sets the tone for your life and where you want to go. Neither of these are comfortable or easy. They take thought and vision. But they are necessary if you want to succeed in your business and at home. This section will show you what these can look like so that you can set your own TODAY.

What Success Means

The definition of success is this: *The accomplishment of an aim or purpose.* Success can look like many things and it really depends on what it looks like for you. If success means staying home with your kids, homeschooling and raising wonderful, well rounded children then do it, Momma! If it means creating a business or working in a business, while working at home with your kids or with your kids being cared for outside the home, that's up to you. To be successful means attaining what you set out to attain. Getting what you wanted to get from the beginning. It means not selling yourself short or giving up when things get challenging. You'll see me using the word "success" a lot throughout the book. What I mean by this word is "accomplishing a purpose", whatever that purpose is for your life. What does success mean to you?

Creating My Why

I started my real estate journey in 2012. I started off "swimming" because the only other choice was to "sink" and I wasn't about to sink. Sinking was not an option. I dove in head first and went for it! I was rocking and rolling, making sales, helping more and more families each year and growing my team. Things were going really well...and then GOD moved in my heart.

As my real estate business grew, I realized that this could mean more for me than just selling houses. It sounds silly because, you guessed it, the main job of a real estate agent is selling houses. But when I realized my calling was bigger than that, I started to examine what I wanted my life to look like. I figured out that I was making a positive impact in people's lives. I was helping them move from one stage of their life to the next. I was the connector between where they were and where they were going. I was assisting them during one of the biggest decisions of their lives. That's where my why was determined. I set out to inspire and support people during this amazing journey because "Changing Homes Changes Lives", this became my team mission statement. The key is that "when I discovered my WHY", the game changed. My vision became bigger, my goals exploded and my mind really began to dream without limits.

There are many WHY reasons. Based on what I have found to be the most common, I have included three to discuss: Happiness, Purpose and Income.

When Your WHY is "Happiness"

Creating your "life priorities" sounds a little intimidating, right? It's a little scary to put your biggest goals down on paper. It's also necessary and the only way to truly map out your plan for the future. While only God knows the many turns our lives will take, it's important to develop a desired path and ask Him to guide your steps.

I recently encouraged my team to write down their life priorities. I then asked my assistant to type them all out, laminate them and distribute them to all the ladies. Now, their priorities are all down on paper. Forever. They took that step, completed the task and now the groundwork is laid out.

As I began thinking about my life priorities, I began to really look inside myself and think about what I wanted to accomplish and fulfill most in life. This is not designed to be a dream list. It's an attainable representation of what you want your life to look life. Whenever you question a choice you are making or feel in a funk, review this list and see if your current decisions are aligning with your life priorities.

I now have mine displayed where I can see them, review them and hold myself accountable. Being vulnerable, I am going to share mine with you. Here they are:

> ➤ *Being a witness to all by the way I live, always remembering that "I am the only Bible some people will ever read"!*

> ➤ *Encouraging other moms and women to go for their goals, dream big and "Do it afraid" through my business, blog, podcast and the way I live my life.*

> ➤ *Raising my children to know the love of God. Demonstrating His love to them through my actions, in my training them and in the way I live intentionally.*

> ➤ *Maintaining a strong and healthy marriage with communication and a constant willingness to improve and make things the best they can be. Having a servant's heart and striving to be a "Proverbs 31 Woman".*

> *Constructing a strong business with solid clients and a great reputation for my hard work, dedication and drive.*

Now, please know that your list is going to look different than mine. We all have unique gifts and abilities. Once you figure out what yours are, you will be better able to create your priorities list.

Also know that I fail sometimes to live up to these priorities. I'm not always a "Proverbs 31" wife...sorry hubby. But this list helps to hold me accountable and makes me strive to be better.

So, go ahead, create your list. Be bold and laminate it so that you cannot go back. It's a small step that will make a big impact on your life.

Rocks, Pebbles & Sand

"Make sure you put the BIG things FIRST." This is something that most people don't understand and therefore, do not do. I am fully convinced that life is all about intentionality. Life should never just happen to us. When we have that mindset, nothing gets accomplished in the way that it should. It's so important to have a firm foundation to base your life on.

Our pastor, Joshua Cossey of Faith Church in Oklahoma City, OK, said these words during church service one week. During this message, he did a demonstration with rocks and sand. In a vase, he stacked up the big rocks first, followed by smaller pebbles and then finally, sand. When the materials were arranged in this manner, everything fit. The foundation was stable, so it had room for the little pebbles and the sand. Lesson- Building your life on a firm foundation (Jesus and his word) allows you to live peacefully and not just survive but thrive!

In the world of motherhood, we have so many things coming at us at once! Raising the kids, working, taking care of the house, grocery shopping, taking care of our husband, planning the kids' schedules and so much more! We do a lot, of that there is no doubt. But if we don't build the framework correctly, things will shift and come toppling down all around us! I see it all the time. Mommas wonder why they cannot make it all fit. They wonder why they cannot find balance. Here are the elements the way that I see them:

- **Big rocks- God and our relationship with him, our marriage and our children, family & close friends. These are the foundation.**

- **Pebbles- Our extended friend list, our kids' schoolwork and activities, our household. These are all very important but must come after the big rocks are solidly placed.**

- **Sand- Grocery shopping, monthly bills, tax time. All the small and sometimes unexpected details that fill up our days. These are always going to happen and sometimes going to pile up.**

In order to balance our lives and wear the many hats that are required of us, we must first make sure our foundation is firm. Here is how to build a strong foundation:

- **Put God first. Sounds simple, right? Give him your life, your future, your career and your family. Know that he will provide and his will is always best.**
- **Start each day with prayer. Start or end with devotional or bible reading. This really does make a difference in each day. It doesn't have to be long or drawn out. But we MUST take a moment to reflect and focus on WHO matters most.**

- **Attend church weekly. "For our family, success begins on Sunday!"**

- **Build a strong marriage. Spend quality time with your spouse. Share secrets, dreams and hopes. Be vulnerable. Become best friends.**

- **Make sure your children know how much you love them and tell them daily! Give them compliments, encourage them and show them you care. If you don't, who will?**

Do these things and you will succeed. Build a firm foundation, prioritize your life and make sure your big rocks, pebbles and sand are in line.

It's Not Just the Dollar Signs

If you are motivated by money, please don't hang your head. Don't you dare do it. Income is what provides for your family and gives you the quality of life you desire. If you're not driven by money, that's okay too. But please don't make those that are feel selfish. I have been called "selfish" and a "workaholic" in my day and I've been told that money cannot buy happiness. While I agree that it most definitely cannot, it can give you a quality of life that you desire and the ability to give in many ways. This is a list I put together for my family and the ways we wanted to use our income:

- ✓ *Tithing at Church*
- ✓ *Donating*
- ✓ *Giving to Those in Need (Friends or strangers)*
- ✓ *Vacationing Each Year with Our Kids*
- ✓ *Ability to Invest and Plan for Our Future*
- ✓ *A Nice Home to Grow Into, Raise Our Family, Hold Gatherings*

I want to break down each of these a little bit further and show you what I mean by each one. Please know we do not have this all figured out or do this perfectly, but this is what has worked for our family and it's nice to look and see where our income goes!

Tithing at church: *Deuteronomy 14:22-26- Make an offering of ten percent, a tithe, of all the produce which grows in your fields year after year. Bring this into the Presence of God, your God, at the place he designates for worship. God will bless you.* I summarized this passage to include keywords that are important here. Tithing is something that is not discussed regularly at church and it should be. Simply put, God calls us to tithe and HE WILL bless us, above and beyond, for our giving. This should be done first and should be the first item on our budgeting list.

Donating: *"When you live like no one else, later you can give like no one else."* That's a famous Dave Ramsey quote. It's very true and also countercultural. If you'll save early on and focus on earning more income for your business, later you'll be able to give and donate to some real cool causes that fuel your heart.

Vacationing: I am a traveler. I love seeing new places. My husband could take it or leave it. We really make it a priority to travel with our kids each year. We take several mini camping trips where we enjoy the outdoors and spend time together. We also do at least one big trip each year. We plan ahead for it and have gotten to see some really amazing places with our kids! I have a map in our home showing all the places we have gone and are planning to go! I get comments on it all the time from guests. It's exhilarating to see the adventures ahead!

Investing and Planning: My husband can geek out on this stuff, seeing that he works in the financial advising field. I just know the basics and am learning more each day. We do a lot of family planning and discussing our best options for investing for our future. I'm not going to discuss the best choices or options here. But I will say that generating an income allows your family to have options when it comes to planning for the future.

Home: Here is my area of expertise. Having a creating a life-giving home is so important to me. We love having a home that we can enjoy and raise our kids in! We also use our home for many gatherings, social events and even hosted a wedding last year. Having a larger home and some land means, for us, that we can bless for people and enjoy providing a place for others to feel included and welcome!

No matter what your why is, or if it's a combination of these or others, just remember that your why is special and specific to you. Only you know the true desires that God has placed in your heart. Trust that He is still continuing a good working in you and will continue it. Know your why, know your purpose.

I Believe
By Ashley

I believe strongly in the power of prayer and hard work.

I believe in treating others well and being kind.

I believe that a home should be life-giving with open doors and plenty of seats at the dinner table.

I believe that marriage should be forever and love should keep growing continually.

I believe that children should get dirty and playing outdoors should be a requirement.

I believe that everyone we meet has a story and a purpose.

I believe that we are all on a journey and only God can determine our final destination.

Discussion Questions:

What are your life priorities?

_____

_____

_____

_____

Write down YOUR WHY right now.

_____

_____

_____

_____

What could you do with more income?

_____

_____

_____

_____

Rising Strong

What Women Say: "I give grace to everyone else except to myself."

What God Says: God, give grace, get me up on my feet. I'll show them a thing or two. Psalm 41:10 (MSG)

Kites rise against the wind- not with it. - Winston Churchill

Practical Tip: *Pick up the house each night. You know what I cannot stand? Waking up to a messy house. I would rather stay up late, after the kids are in bed and do a pick-up than wake up feeling overwhelmed with it. I have learned to give myself 15 minutes every evening after the kids are in bed in order to do a quick clean. That includes picking up toys, putting the throw pillows back on the couch and clearing off the kitchen counters. By doing this, I can go to bed with my to-do list checked off and wake up with a fresh start and clear mind!*

Goal of This Chapter: *The goal of this chapter is to show you how amazing you are and how special it is to be a mom. Being a Mompreneur is the best of the both worlds and I want to tell you why! This chapter will also help you learn how to allow faith to fuel your life and create balance as you strive to "do it all".*

The Harvest

The Law of the harvest applies in farming, as the crops are sown and eventually reaped, and it applies in life. We get out of life what we put into it. As the old saying goes "you reap what you sow". You cannot expect to have a flourishing business or wonderful kids if you don't put the time and effort into both. Both take consistency, ambition and determination. Both take patience, intentionality and desire. If you want well-adjusted, well-behaved, loving children: pray for them, spend time with them, tell them you love them and do everything in love. If you want a successful business: Pray for it, work on it without ceasing, treat your clients right and show them your appreciation. If you want to warn a good reputation, treat people right and be kind. The hard work comes now, the reward comes later.

Pray for Favor

When I first started in my business, wow, I prayed for God's favor A LOT. Like every time I prayed. I prayed that God would bless my little business and that he would use me for his glory. I prayed that he would show himself mighty through me. And He never failed to do just that. Over and over again, I have seen his hand at work. I have seen things work that never should have worked out. I have seen plans succeed that should have failed. I have seen God piece together things that should have remained a puzzle. God's favor truly creates miracles to those who pray for it!

The Best of Both Worlds

Being a Mompreneur is wonderful. It's tough. It's great. It's trying. In this role, we are not a full-time 8:00 - 5:00 employee, yet we are not full-time stay-at-home moms either. We blend both worlds into some kind of controlled chaos. I recently posted a picture of me working on a contract while in the airport getting ready to leave for a trip, while also, you guessed it, feeding babies and refereeing toddlers! Just another day in paradise.

Here are the reasons why I love what I do:

1) I feel that I get to give 100% in all areas. My kids, husband, home and career all get my time and I can accomplish this while giving time and care in all areas. This does not mean each gets 100% daily. Some days, my kids get 90% of my energy, other days, I am working on my business and it takes up most of my day. But you know what? That's okay. Even on these days where the scale tips heavily to one side, I know the other side is taken care of because I have invested my time wisely during other days.

2) I make my own schedule. My schedule does not control me. I work when I want to, vacation when I want to and plan my schedule around my life.

3) I can keep up with my home and do the things I love because of my lifestyle. My hard work allows me to achieve, set goals and reach summits. This gives me the freedom to make smart financial choices, investments and try new things!

While all these things are grand and I honestly would not change my life for the world, there are definitely days that are hard and it's not for everyone. Here are the reasons why it's challenging:

1) I'm needed in all areas. Without a babysitter close by and my husband working full-time, I am my kids' everything. Caretaker, scheduler, chauffeur, teacher, coach, you name it. I know many moms can relate to this!

2) I am often working with a baby in my lap. Some days, well a lot of days, are spent sending emails, writing contracts and doing paperwork with a baby on my lap, a child talking in my ear while getting sippy cups and emptying the dishwasher, all at once. I kid you not. If you want to be a Mompreneur, you better be a multi-tasker.

3) Sometimes I just want to work. Sometimes I have so much I need to do but my family comes first. Always. My kids are able to help me sometimes and it's great for them to see what Momma does. But I cannot just hop up and get in the grind! My husband just told me yesterday (after being on a trip with our three kids for over a week) that being home with the kids all day is WAY harder than going into the office! Ha!

With all this being said, is there anything better than being a Mompreneur? We get to run our businesses while raising our babies and it brings so much joy on both sides! I am super thankful for my career in real estate! It has helped me achieve great heights, helped so many people find new homes (over 200 in 5 years) and allowed me to fulfill God's calling on my life! I'll be sharing some of my favorite books that have helped me in my journey. I hope they help you too!

My advice for all mompreneurs would be: DO YOUR BEST, WORK HARD and HAVE FAITH.

Running On Faith

In business and in life, we are all really just running on faith. When you own your own business as I do, there are no guaranteed paychecks, no clients given to me, nothing that says my next few months or the year ahead will be successful. It's all a matter of faith, hard work and determination.

We have nothing to guarantee our children will be safe, healthy and able to endure each new day. We simply have to trust God with our family's safety, health and futures! That's easy to say but sometimes hard to truly live. This is scary, uncomfortable and just plain uncommon. Our families were given to us by God so we must give them back to Him. Our businesses were inspired and brought into fruition by God so we must give Him our trust and allow him to work within us.

Hebrews 11:1 says "Faith is the substance of things hoped for and the evidence of things not seen."

This is one of my favorite verses in The Bible. It proves that God has called us to live a life of faith. Faith is not easy but it's so worth it. When you have faith, you can have peace and know that "God's got this".

I've read shirts that say, "I'm just winging it". That may be true, but it really comes down to the fact that God's in control. And when he's in control, we can live an intentional life.

These are the reasons I enjoy living a faith-filled life:

1) There is no need to worry or stress. God is in control anyway. Pray, do what he has called you to do and he will take care of the rest.
2) God will go above and beyond your wildest dreams if you just allow Him to have free reign over your entire life. He knows best anyway.
3) We are weak, but He is strong. What can I accomplish without Him, anyhow? I choose to put my faith in the One who holds the World in His hands.

This one can be hard to hear. But here it is. In my opinion, here is what living a faith-filled life does NOT mean:

1) You do not get to pray and wait. You have to act. Pray and then go.
2) God provides to those who act in faith.
3) Work for what you want. Let God guide your path.

If your faith is having a tough time and you struggle with doubt, I encourage you to listen to these songs. Here are the lyrics:

On the mountains, I will bow my life to the one who set me there.
In the valley, I will lift my eyes to the one who sees me there.
When I'm standing on the mountain aft, didn't get there on my own.
When I'm walking through the valley end, no I am not alone!

You're God of the hills and valleys!
Hills and Valleys!
God of the hills and valleys
And I am not alone!
-Song by Tauren Wells

If you've got pain, He's a pain taker.
If you feel lost, He's a way maker.
If you need freedom and saving, He's a prison-
shaking Savior.
If you've got chains, He's a chain breaker.
-Song by Zach Williams

So, realize the importance of turning over your business and your family to Him. I encourage you to live a life of faith TODAY.

ADVERSITY

As I have grown in my sphere of influence who I am deep down has not changed. I want to be liked by people. I wish I were not this way but it's the way God created me. I care about people's feelings and their thoughts, even their thoughts about me. But I've learned that some people are just not going to like you, no matter what you do. We must understand that adversity is always hard until we get to the other side of it.

DOING IT ALL

"How in the world do you do it all"? I get asked this question really often. Here's the short answer. "I don't." I literally and physically cannot do it all. That's why I put systems in place to make sure everything is taken care of without me having to do it all. I now have two assistants who help me with work tasks to ensure my team members are on-point and have all the back-up needed. They also ensure my clients have great care, access to the right resources and feel super appreciated. They keep me on-task and make sure all the details are taken care of. I'm not good at details and I know this about myself. Therefore, I know I must hire people who are good at details and who those things come naturally for in their daily lives!

I also have a personal assistant who helps me around my home, doing tasks like laundry and keeping my home picked up. This is a recent development but it's been something that has allowed me to spend time in other areas.

I have a friend who is stylist and goes shopping with me to help me pick out new outfits so that I look good when speaking in front of people. I have a friend who is a home designer who helps me make interior choices for my home when decorating. I have a business coach who meets with me monthly to help me with my goals, business decisions and planning. I have a relationship coach who helps me mend and repair relationships and create healthy ones. I have an accountability partner who I meet with monthly who allows me to vent, lets me ask questions and needs me to answer some for her. I have a few babysitters on hand whom I can call when I need a few hours away to work or to go to an appointment. Even to go on a scheduled date night with my husband. These are all people that I utilize regularly to help make me the best me possible. Do they magically appear? No. Do they maintain themselves? No. Are they worth it? Absolutely!

It's so important to have people in your life who can help you in different areas. People who can fill in your gaps so you can live fully and whole, confident and sure, ready for anything! Don't be ashamed of that. Be proud, girl. You are working hard to create the life you want. And that means entrusting others to help you. And, in turn, you help them as well.

The Truth About Mean Girls

Mean girls - we have all dealt with them. They are in every school, every corner, no matter where you grew up. And sadly, they still exist even after high school. They are the girls who laugh behind your back, gossip to make themselves feel better and try to bring you down. What's funny about mean girls is that in high school they seem to "rule the school". But those are their only glory days and the days ahead for them, won't look so bright. In life and in business, you'll have these types of people again and again. Don't worry about them. Just be you and use the gifts God gave you to accomplish the mission He placed in your heart. Someday you will look back and smile from the mountain top. And those girls? They will be nowhere to be seen.

Give God Your Gifts

When you tell God to use you, He will put a microphone in your hand. It's scary to pray bold prayers, right? When I pray boldly, I know that I better be ready for a breakthrough and for something "scary" to occur. God is not into safety nets. When we pray for His favor and for Him to use us, be ready to be thrown into some scary situations. He cares too much for us to let us live complacent lives. He wants us to live daring lives, praying bold prayers and making courageous moves. If we allow Him, He will open the doors. We only need to step through the threshold.

God opens doors no one can shut, when it's His will and His plan. When you walk in bravery and not in defeat, a new world opens up for you. Don't be afraid of what lies ahead. Instead, be afraid of not trying.

What if God is so good that He allows us to be tried and tested so that we can get to the other side. So that our character may be developed. So that we may become better leaders. So that He can get glory. I believe He is that good.

Every time I go through a "character building" trial, that's what I'm calling it. What it really means is "a really hard time where you feel like you don't know what you're made of anymore". Every time I'm in the middle of one of these times, I think "this is hard. I don't like it. It hurts. I just want this to be over. And I ask God why." When I'm on the other side of it, I can easily see the why behind the trial. My character grew a lot during that time. I really figured out who I am and most importantly, how good God is. I gained confidence. My weaknesses became my strengths.

Though the cherry trees don't blossom and the strawberries don't ripen, though the apples are worm-eaten and the wheat fields are stunted, Though the sheep pens are sheepless and the cattle barns are empty, I'm singing joyful praise to God. I'm turning cartwheels of joy to my Savior God. Counting on God's rule to prevail, I take heart and gain strength. I run like a deer. I feel like I'm king of the mountain!
Habakkuh 3:17-19

Discussion Questions:

How have people disappointed you?

_____

_____

_____

_____

What have been some of your biggest struggles?

_____

_____

_____

_____

How can your faith be bigger than your fear?

_____

_____

_____

_____

Speaking Life

What Women Say: "I constantly feel like I'm failing and that leads to worry."

What God Says: "Don't fret or worry. Instead of worrying, pray. Let petitions and praises shape your worries into prayers, letting God know your concerns. Before you know it, a sense of God's wholeness, everything coming together for good, will come and settle you down. It's wonderful what happens when Christ displaces worry at the center of your life." Philippians 4:6 (MSG)

"Little people want to keep you little." - John Maxwell

Practical Tip #3: *Empty your sink every single night. Do your dishes right after dinnertime so you will then have time to spend quality moments with your family before bedtime. By emptying your sink, putting dishes in the dishwasher, wiping down your counters and lighting a candle, you will feel more confident, settled and peaceful.*

Goal of This Chapter

The goal of this chapter is to help you say goodbye to negativity and eliminate it from your life. We often don't want to let people or things go that cause us pain because we are afraid. We are afraid of what it will look like to say "goodbye". I want to ensure you that some relationships, poisonous situations and things need to be let go of, I'll show you why.

When People Don't Get it

This is one of the toughest chapters to write, because it's real and it's painful. It's also the easiest because I have experienced every emotion, felt devastation and betrayal as I've risen and girl, I've lived to tell about it.

This may sound mean, rude or cynical, but you need to hear it, so here it is. Not everyone is going to be okay with your WHY. Let me say it again for those of you in the back. Not everyone is going to be okay with WHY, your calling, your decisions. Those closest to you are probably not going to "get it". That includes your family and perhaps, friends who are closest to you. Here is the catch- you have you to okay with that. You have to be okay with it because you have no other choice. You will be forced to look deep inside yourself, develop some thick skin and move forward in faith and perseverance. If there is one thing I know, it's "If God brings you to it, He will get you through it." Can I get an Amen?

Let me jump in and say this. I do think you need the support of your spouse. If I didn't have my husband to talk through things with me, I would not have been able to succeed at the level that I have. He is an encourager, a supporter, even when others may oppose. Sometimes, he has to reign me in. I tend to say "yes" to too many things. You know about the "free spirit" and the "nerd" that Dave Ramsey talks about in relationships. I am the free spirit. I often joke with my husband that I make sure his life is fun! Without me, he would say "no" to too many things". We balance each other well in this way. If your spouse doesn't get it, you need to have a serious discussion and get on the same page. Your future depends on this.

When I first started seeing some success in business, I was surprised that I did not feel the support from family that I expected to feel. I felt like I couldn't be proud, like I had to take myself down a level to make others more comfortable. And I did for a while. It wasn't right and it didn't do anyone any good. Sometimes family and old friends view you in a light of how you used to be, how you grew up and how you used to live. They have a tough time seeing you in the light of how you are now. Even Jesus faced this when he grew up and began his ministry. His family still saw him as the little boy Jesus, the son of the carpenter, the one who grew up in Nazareth. How was this ordinary boy now a man who healed many and performed miracles? Jesus was finally living His calling; the calling God had destined for Him since before he was born in that stable to his mother Mary. Jesus had grown up and He was ready to live the full life God had for Him. What would have happened if he had shrunk back and only lived partially, to a standard that made those around Him more comfortable? Well, number one, God would have been disappointed in Him because His purpose and his full potential had not been met. Number two, the world would have never known what true love looks like and generations would have been negatively affected.

Instead, Jesus chose to boldly live AND die according to God's purpose for his life. This was not a life of comfort, but a life of risk and uncertainty. He could only be certain of this- God loved Him and He had great plans for Him. What would happen if we looked at our own lives and journeys in the same way? What would happen if we stopped trying to live in way that made everyone around us more comfortable? What if we decided to fully live the life God called us to live? No, history will not be forever changed and generations impacted because well, we aren't Jesus. But we could change our family tree, the lives of our children, the lives of those we influence. We could make a difference in our small part of the world, just by doing what God created us to do in the first place. Live boldly, live bravely, live in a world without comfort zones.

Pruning

Every branch in me that does not bear fruit, He takes it away; and every branch that bears fruit, He prunes it so that it may bear more fruit. John 15:2 (New American Standard Bible.)

God has to prune you to help you grow and make you the most effective. Pruning is never fun, it hurts sometimes. It's necessary. In order to grow taller, go higher and reach more people, some relationships must be ended. Maybe that's those that are: negative, unhealthy or make you feel like you can fully be yourself.

Don't make yourself small so others feel more comfortable. -Rachel Hollis

I had to realize this in one of my relationships with a girlfriend. I had a friend who was constantly negative, who I was always needing to uplift and who judged me and my leadership qualities at every chance she got. This was not always apparent. Sometimes I even thought "It's no big deal", but it was a big deal. Even if she didn't speak these negative words out loud, her behavior and attitude poured out and came through in her disposition and the influence it had on those I was working to inspire was tangible. Once I realized it was okay to let the friendship go, a whole new world opened up. I had to fully realize this---Not everyone deserves access to your life. Rewind and repeat. Not everyone deserves access to your life.

If someone in your life is bringing you down or even trying to privately cut you down, it's time to cut them out. Clean house, girlfriend. Even if the size of your circle needs to decrease, at least the quality of that circle will increase.

You want friends, team members, employees and those you surround yourself with to clap when you win. In return, you want to celebrate their accomplishments. Once you let go of those negative relationships, now can your life improve for the better.

Speaking Life

As I think about what has helped me most in created a business and a life that I want, I realized that I have learned the value of "speaking life". Here are the four key areas that I do this:

➢ *Speak Life Into Myself*

➢ *Speak Life Into My Family*

➢ *Speak Life Into Others*

➢ *Have Life Spoken Into Me*

Speak Life Into Myself

Wouldn't it be great if we all had faith like a child? I'm sure you have seen your kids' imaginations and the way their options are limitless in their minds. My son, who is 5, goes between wanting to be a Superhero and a Ninja Turtle, depending on the day. He has no concept that this is impossible, that Super Heroes don't really exist, that Superman and Spiderman aren't real or that the world will change him by the time he is a teenager. The world will tell him that he has to choose something realistic eventually, but right now, I will let him go on believing that he can be a superhero! Here are some things I hear my five-year-old say to himself: I am strong. I am so brave. I fight the bad guys. No one can stop me. I help people!

Wow. Just wow. I know this is totally in a fictional sense that he says to himself as he fights the bad guys, but just think with me for a moment. What if we spoke like this over our life as we lived each day? Imagine this- What if we woke up each morning and repeated these affirmations? I am strong. I am brave. I fight against wrongdoing. No one can stop me because I have set my mind toward my goals. I help people and love what I do!

If we said these things to ourselves daily, do you think it would change how we pursue each day? I do.

Here is a small thing we can do to accomplish this. Write a note card with a verse, note, or word of encouragement for yourself. It can be something that speaks specifically to you- something that maybe only you know. Put it somewhere that you will see every day. I have mine taped to my bathroom mirror. Maybe you can put yours in the visor in your car or in your wallet. This will serve as a daily reminder of what you want your mind to be filled with and what you want to become.

If you don't have a dream that scares the living daylight out of you, you're not dreaming big enough. I encourage you to write down your dreams, even the scary ones. The ones that you are afraid to show anyone because they will think you have gone crazy.

Speak Life Into My Family

I have a two-year-old son. He's your typical two-year-old wild boy. He's into everything. I can't turn around without him getting into something, pouring something out making a mess somewhere across the house. Just a few weeks ago, he managed to flood the laundry room, dump out my spice cabinet, use a Sharpie to put a new shade on my white cabinets and squirt toothpaste across the bathroom. And this was just in one weekend. Oh, the joys of raising boys!

Here's the deal- I've been speaking life into this book. I have been speaking over him what I want him to become. I can't say to him "you are such a bad little boy. Why do you not listen? You act like a little crazy person!" That's what I want to say. Help me, Jesus! Instead, after some serious corrections and punishment, I look him in the eyes and hug him. I tell him these things: "You are such a sweet boy. You are a good listener. I know you like to do good and make mommy proud. You are so thoughtful. You are my little boy and I love you." Sometimes I laugh while I'm saying these words. But I'm saying these things because that's who I want him to become. I want my son, all my kids, to be thoughtful, good listeners and sweet. And above all else, in the middle of the messes, I want them to know that Mommy loves them.

I had a client who spoke negativity over our entire transaction. While we were house hunting, I kept hearing the same phrases come from her lips. Phrases that spoke defeat. "Bad things always happen to me." "I have the worst luck." "I shouldn't even try because nothing ever goes right." Oh boy. I was supposed to help this person buy a new home. And she lacked a lot of confidence. In case you didn't know, being a Realtor is truly about 80% counseling services. I gave pep talks, words of encouragement and listened to melt-downs. But, by golly, how much easier would it have been if my client, Mary, would have trusted me and trusted the process. If she would have spoken life over her situation. If she would have walked in faith knowing that God had the right house out there for her? If Mary would have known this and believed it, she would have saved herself a lot of stress. Because, what we speak over ourselves is who we become. And what we speak over our circumstance becomes our outcome.

So, speak life, speak life
To the deadest darkest night
Speak life, speak life
When the sun won't shine and you don't know why
Look into the eyes of the broken hearted
Watch them come alive as soon as you speak hope
You speak love, you speak
You speak life

Speak Life Into Others

We each have a unique opportunity to speak life into other people. As Moms and business owners, we have such a unique opportunity. You are viewed as influencers who have impact and people watch you, they listen to your words more than you know. When I want people to know their worth and their value to me, I try to make that visible, audible and tangible. I think a great way I can explain this is the way I take care of my clients. In real estate, I want to create clients for life. I don't want to be the Realtor who you work with and then forget their name a few months later. I promise you, if I work with you, you will never forget my name. The reason? You will be put on my list that I have carefully crafted and you will hear from me throughout the year in several ways.

Through personal notes - I am a big believer in the written word. I know the value in expressing thoughts and feelings through a little note and the impact it can make on someone. My clients will always receive a birthday card, home anniversary card and a few "just because" cards throughout each year. I do these at the beginning of each month and it's non-negotiable.

Through personal touches - My team creates "pop by" gifts that we deliver to our clients and friends throughout the year. These are just little things that show people we care and are thinking of them. For Easter each year, we deliver chocolate bunnies to our clients' homes and for the beginning of football season, we mail OU/OSU schedules to each household in our sphere. Is this easy to do all this? No. Does it take planning and work. Yes. Is it worth it? Absolutely.

Through events - My team hosts several events each year that I invite my clients to be a part of. One of these is a client appreciation event where we invite all past, current and future clients to join us to be celebrated! We also host a Mother's Day Brunch for all the Moms in our sphere to feel loved and celebrated. This year, I'm also adding a Women's Empowerment Event where we will hold a self-defense class at my office. We will also be doing Santa Pictures for our clients and friends at the end of the year. You may ask- What does all this have to do with Real Estate? Well, this all goes back to "my why". My way is to reach people. By being relatable and helping others, it's all a cycle. I want to take care of my people. By doing this, I am able to run a 100% referral business. I buy ZERO leads. If you know the real estate industry, you know this is very unheard of for successful agents. But here is the deal- I don't want to buy leads and work with clients who I have to fight for. I want to create "raving fans" and get clients who come to me- ready to work with me, who understand my purpose, who respect me and who are bought in.

Have Life Spoken Into Me

Sometimes, I think this is the hardest area because we put ourselves last. Why is this? We want to take care of everyone else but not us. Let's change that! You MUST have life spoken into you. Here are a few things I recommend.

Have devotional time- This may be Bible reading, journaling or devotional reading. Try to find a time each day to do this and you will see a difference immediately. Also find time for prayer. Mine is often while I'm driving in my car. There is no place that is too far or too hard to talk to God.

Listen to podcasts- Make a list of podcasts that will encourage you and motivate you. There are so many out there. Many that relate to your specific industry. Ask friends which ones they like and get them loaded up on your phone.

Make a playlist- Get some music that will inspire you and pump you up when needed.

Have a reading list- I love paperback books. I like to have them spread in a few places so I can pick one up wherever I am. By my nightstand, by my recliner and in my car. Let books speak wisdom into you and learn from what others have written.

Find inspiration- Find a place where you find inspiration- For me, that's nature. Being outdoors and in nature makes me feel alive and inspires me. I feel inspired to write, create and be my best self.

Strength From Struggle
by Ashley

The higher you rise, the more people will want to take you down.

You can either accept defeat or obtain victory, but you can't do both.

Strength comes from experiencing weakness, hurt and deprivation.

The more we grow, the more it's going to hurt. It's all a process.

People will disappoint you and let you down. God will always know what's best and be two steps ahead.

Discussion Questions:

How can you speak life in these four ways?

_____

_____

_____

_____

Do you have things that need to be pruned from your life?

_____

_____

_____

_____

How will letting go of negativity allow you to flourish?

_____

_____

_____

_____

Don't Miss the Magic

What Women Say: "I want to be confident and sure, instead of anxious."

What God Says: "But blessed is the man who trusts me, God, the woman who sticks with God. They're like trees re-planted in Eden putting down roots near the rivers." Jeremiah 17:7 (MSG)

Practical Tip: *Start your day off with a prayer, a reading in your devotional and some affirming words. End your day in the same way.*

The Goal of This Chapter: *The goal of this chapter is to show you the magic that is all around you each day! By looking for joy, you will find it in the everyday moments and the most unexpected ways.*

The Magic of Moments

It recently snowed at our house. In Oklahoma, we get about three snows per year if we're lucky. It's actually really nice because it blows in and the kids get to play and enjoy it, and then it warms up and melts and it's gone! On this particular snowy day, it was cold and wet and just downright yucky. My kids didn't care. They wanted to go outside and play in it, build a snowman, they thought it was beautiful. I, on the other hand, was frustrated. I had things to do. Errands to run, a workout to accomplish, tasks to check off my to-do list. And you know what? I totally missed the magic of a snow day. Through a child's eyes, a snow day is magical. As a mom, we see the muddy shoes coming through the door that we will have to clean up.

We see a day stuck inside while life passes us by outside. We see the mess. Our kids see the miracle.

As I pondered this that night after the kids were asleep, I realized that I had totally missed the fun of the snow day. I hadn't gone outside one time to play with my kids. I was aggravated all day because it was yucky. I didn't even appreciate the beauty of ice-covered trees and huge snowflakes falling from the sky. I missed the amazement of seeing everything turn white. I focused on the mess.

The next morning, I awoke early, bundled my kids up and we went outside to play in the snow. I strapped the baby on me and he got to experience his first snow! I watched the kids make snow angels and slide down hills. I took pictures of some breathtaking sights as the snow and ice shone from the trees. I enjoyed the beauty and serenity of it all! I made snow ice cream for the kids. I reveled in the moments and I loved it.

I learned something during that snowstorm. Sometimes those messy moments, those inconvenient times, the long days, those are the times we really need to step back, count our blessings and enjoy the moments.

The Magic of JOY

I'm in my 30s now. I have never really thought about this concept until this year and it's changing my life.

"Do more of the things that bring you joy."

I made a list of things that bring me joy and a list of things that take my joy away.

On the things that take it away, I have delegated those tasks or found a way to eliminate them.

By eliminating these things, I am able to focus on the things that bring me joy, I am able to work on the things in which I excel, I am able to be the best me for myself, for God, for my kids and for my clients. I am able to plan, dream and create.

My inspiration is soaring this year and my joy is increasing each day. Like everything else, making this happen is a decision. CHOOSE joy each day.

Here is what my list looked like:

What brings me joy: Spending quality time with my family, being outdoors, reading, writing, working, cooking.

What takes my joy away: vacuuming, laundry, grocery shopping, meal planning, bathroom cleaning, organizing closets, constantly trying to go on a date night and scrambling for a babysitter.

When I wrote this and read it back to myself, it suddenly became clear to me what I needed to do. I needed to ask for help. I know most moms understand this. When you have children, it becomes more difficult to keep a clean home, an organized home, a stocked pantry and empty laundry baskets. It becomes a struggle to feel caught up.

What would I do if I could eliminate the "joy stealers": I would focus on what's important- my family, my career and my dreams. When I am at home, I want to play with my kids, not be cleaning around them constantly.

When you get to a point where you can, delegate the things that don't bring you joy. I learned early in my career that you cannot do everything well, but you can do some things better than anyone else. Because of this, I focus on this principle when delegating: "Only do what only you can do". That means, the things that I do not need to be involved in, the things I can give away, the things that someone else can do better, I should let someone else do them. Here are some myths I have learned along the way:

- *If I give this job to someone else, they won't enjoy the work.*

- *I am lazy if I give work away.*

- *I am arrogant if I allow someone else to do this work for me.*

Wrong, wrong, wrong. Someone else will be blessed by the work you provide for them. By giving them a job, even a part-time job, you can help provide security for another person's family. I have given jobs to several woman, all in part-time roles. Some are for my real estate business, some are cleaning jobs (either at my home or one of our investment properties), my personal household or babysitting. These jobs are all meaningful. By providing them to someone else, I not only helped them by providing monetary support, I increased my ability to do other things.

My business coach once gave me some good advice on this subject. When I asked her if she thought I was selfish or silly for hiring women to fill roles in my life where I left gaps, she looked at me earnestly and smiled. "When you help others succeed and provide opportunities for me, you are being a good steward of what God has given you", she said. I had never thought of it quite that way. The amazing part is- they were helping me and I was helping them. Everyone came out ahead.

When I hired my Transaction Coordination and eventually, my Marketing Specialist, it freed up so much time for me. I was able to focus more on my clients, on growing my business, recruiting new agents and brainstorming new ideas. Those are things my staff members would not feel comfortable doing. They could not do them at my level. On the same token, I couldn't input data and do all the behind-the scenes work that they do at their level. It's their skill set and they are proud for the work. They are blessed by the compensation, the title and the ability to be a part of something important.

Bringing on a Personal Assistant to help with some of the household chores was an amazing asset. By doing so, I was able to come home to a clean, organized home, without feel overwhelmed at the work I had ahead of me. The daunting tasks that were sucking my time and energy away were no longer looming over my head. They were done and I felt free. Free to play, free to sit, free to read, free to do what I wanted, not what I felt I needed. Free to be the Mom I should have been all along. By saying no to doing more, I really said yes to more life!

If you need a babysitter once a month so you and your husband can have a date night, do it, commit to it, put it on the calendar. If you need someone to help you with grocery shopping, paying bills, cleaning or your workload, find the right person. Take a step of faith. There is someone waiting to answer that calling for you and God knows just who it is. **Give a blessing, be a blessing, receive a blessing.**

The Magic of No Excuses

What I hear most often from women who want to succeed but cannot seem to get their start is this: excuses. I am fully confident that you cannot be successful and full of excuses simultaneously. You must pick a side. Some excuses may be:

- *I'm too busy to get started.*
- *I don't have enough hours in the day.*
- *I'm not qualified.*
- *I'm not a people-person.*
- *I just don't have the eagerness.*
- *No one cares what I do.*

Here's the truth. Whether you think you can or you think you can't, you're right. You can do whatever you make your mind up that you can do. If you fully believe in what you are trying to accomplish and you have prayerfully asked God for his favor, watch out world.

I remember during my second year in Real Estate, I was trying to hit a goal. It was a highly-coveted goal and one that not too many agents achieve, especially second-year agents. But I made it my goal to hit this and by golly, I was gonna do it. When we got to December, I was five houses away from doing this. That meant, I had to sell five houses in one month in order to hit the mark. December is, by far, the most difficult month to sell homes. People are thinking about Christmas, they are preparing for parties, they are looking forward to breaks and vacations. You get the point. They aren't thinking about buying houses. But I was not about to go down without a fight. I told my husband "Babe, all I have to do is sell 5 houses in December and I've got this!" "Is that all?" he laughed. "Watch me", I replied. I worked my tail off that month, with as much eagerness and tenacity as I had inside me. I worked my listings, I sat on open houses, I made phone calls as much as I could and, by the grace of God, I sold those five houses that month. I hit my goal and surpassed it by $8. Was it easy? Heck no! Was it worth it? Absolutely. Could I have given myself a break and said "better luck next year"? For sure. But this was not my calling and I got into this business to succeed. By not making excuses and pushing through the pain, I accepted my award filled with so much happiness that I wanted to cry. Hard work really does pay off. To this day, I still wear that lapel pin and display that trophy. I'll never forget the long days and nights I spent to earn that. But it wasn't about the trophy. It was about proving to myself that I could do it. My lapel pin just displays that. It says "$100,000 Club".

The Magic of No Regrets

Through all the craziness, we have really learned that you cannot let other people's opinions, thoughts or words define your life. Your destiny is between you and God. When you know what you want, you must go after it with all you have and not worry about your critics. They will always be there. What really matters is that you won't look back and regret what you didn't do.

I cannot imagine what my life would look life if had run away from the risks that we presented to me. All the good things I have experienced in life- my marriage, my children, my career, this book- it all stems back to taking risks. And the greater the risk, the greater the reward!

Taking risks and living boldly and with intention is really the only way to live. I've been known to do things that the world may consider crazy and I'm not done yet. I write down big dreams in a little notebook, for my eyes only. These are dreams that are big and crazy and maybe silly, but that's okay, because they are mine. If someone were to find and read this little notebook, they would probably think I am nuts. But, if we don't dream and make big plans for our lives, we will get stuck in a mediocrity mindset. By living in a way that you will conquer whatever life throws at you, you'll get good at making things happen.

"Do one thing each day that scares you." - Eleanor Roosevelt

While writing this book, my time has been limited. I had to find one hour each day when I could write. There was no such extra hour available. So, I created an extra hour in there. 10:00 p.m. - 12:00 a.m. Those were my open hours each day when I could write. The house was quiet, everyone else was asleep and while I would normally be sleeping, I made a commitment to myself to spend those precious hours putting words on paper. My husband always comments that I should get up earlier. However, #1: I am not a morning person and my brain is not its sharpest in the early hours of the day. #2: I am up with the baby and toddler multiple times per night and the idea of dragging myself out of bed when I have just fallen into precious slumber is not just illogical for my life right now, it's dumb. The remainder of my day is spent taking care of my kids, taking care of my home, working at the office or through phone and e-mail and balancing all the plates as they go spinning. But, you know, an amazing thing happens at 10:00 p.m. People stop texting, few emails come through and the world becomes quieter. I had to determine what I really wanted, set a deadline and make it happen. It has not been easy to find this extra time and dedicate myself fully to it, but I did it because it's worth it.

BECAUSE I'M NOT
by Ashley

When we hear "I am not, I cannot and I do not...God says "You are, you can and you will."

I changed all the things I get frustrated with about myself and turned them into positives.

Because I am not a perfectionist, I can multi-task really well and get a lot accomplished. Sometimes I wish I were more into the details, but I'm just not. I'm into getting things done!

Because my makeup is not always on-point and my hair is not flawless, I can get ready pretty quickly and conquer each day. It is the imperfections that make us real.

Because my daily diet isn't always super clean, I can enjoy my favorite foods without feeling guilty. Hey y'all, life is meant to be enjoyed!

Because I am not reserved, I can make friends very easily. I can also connect people and make them feel loved and welcome. Everyone needs to feel needed!

Because I am not afraid, I can be strong.

Because I am not enough, God becomes enough and works through me. His power is made perfect through my weakness. (2 Corinthians 12:9)

Because I am not the perfect mom, I am the perfect mom for my kids.
After all, we are all just a work in progress.

Discussion Questions

What magical moments are you missing because you're so focused on the messes?

_____

_____

_____

_____

How can you appreciate the magical moments?

_____

_____

_____

_____

What can you give away in order to bring more joy into your life?

_____

_____

_____

_____

Losing Isn't Pretty

What Women Say: "I feel like every time I take a step forward, I get knocked two steps back. Maybe I'm not supposed to do anything special."

What God Says: "Who knows? Maybe you were made queen for just such a time as this?" Esther 4:12 (MSG)

"I've missed more than 9,000 shots in my career. I've lost almost 300 games. 26 times, I've been trusted to take the game winning shot and missed. I've failed over and over and over again in my life and that is why I succeed." – Michael Jordan

Practical Tip: *Go for a walk every day. Get your body moving, your blood flowing and spends some time outdoors. This will reset your mind and give your body the healthy boost it desires!*

The Goal of this Chapter: *The goal of this chapter is to show you that we all lose sometimes and it's in those moments, we learn how to win. I don't often share stories of failure. They make me feel embarrassed and I don't like to think back on the painful times. But opening up and sharing those times with others gives the opportunities for them to say "me too". I hope some of these stories will be "me too" moments for you.*

God always has spectacular timing. What's weird about timing is that we don't even understand it until that time has passed and we can look back and see the truth. We can see God's footprints. Looking back, there were definitely one set of footprints in the sand in many times of my life. God has carried me through and held my hand far more times than I can count. In case you have never heard this amazing poem about footprints in the sand, here it is:

One night I dreamed a dream.
As I was walking along the beach with my Lord.
Across the dark sky flashed scenes from my life.
For each scene, I noticed two sets of footprints in the sand,
One belonging to me and one to my Lord.
After the last scene of my life flashed before me,
I looked back at the footprints in the sand.
I noticed that at many times along the path of my life,
especially at the very lowest and saddest time,
there was only one set of footprints.
This really troubled me, so I asked the Lord about it.
"Lord, you said once I decided to follow you,
You'd walk with me all the way.
But I noticed that during the saddest and most troublesome times of my life,
there was only one set of footprints.
I don't understand why, when I need You the most,
You would leave me."
He whispered, "My precious child, I love you and will never leave you, ever, ever.
During your trials and testings,
When you saw only one set of footprints,
It was then that I carried you."

Growing Up Sweating

I spent my whole childhood as an athlete. I was a devoted basketball player. I also played softball and did cheerleading in high school. In softball, I was always the pitcher, both in fast-pitch and slow-pitch. I always wanted to be in the position that had the most action, required the most pressure and had the most to lose. But basketball, that was my main sport. It was the thing I woke up to do each day, practiced in every spare moment and set high goals to make achievements. I was the point guard and shooting guard throughout my 18 years of playing. I played during the school year and then in the off-season, I was either playing with AAU or at summer camp improving my skills. I wanted to play in college so bad. It's what I had spent my whole life working toward. With a high-scoring average and all the accolades came a lot of jealousy and mean girls. It also came with pressure and lots of nights spent crying after games because I didn't play well enough or score enough points. I worked so hard during my school career. I wanted to keep playing and make everyone proud, especially my family who wanted it so badly for me. But after some offers to walk-on as a freshman or move out-of-state to play at a small school, I decided I was done.

I was done with the stress and I no longer had love for the game like I used to. I didn't look forward to playing. It became a dull routine and I dreaded it. I made the choice to say no because I wanted to experience more in college that just a basketball gym. I know I let people down when I chose not to play at the next level, my parents, family and coaches. I worried that I was wasting my talent and the thousands of hours spent in the gym with my mom in the stands. It was a tough decision but I felt a peace about it. The way I saw it, I already knew I could play basketball and be a stand-out. I wanted to see what else I could do, what else I could experience, what else I could become. Looking back on this now, I realize that playing sports taught me so much about life. They taught me how to work really hard to accomplish the goals I wanted. They taught me not to back down when I was afraid or felt inferior. They taught me that losing teaches you more than winning ever can. I learned how to be coached and take correction, how to be a leader and command respect.

The lessons learned while playing sports are so applicable to life. I was always the most determined, the hardest worker and the most committed on my team. I wanted to win and it was never "just a game" to me. I'm so glad I had the opportunity to play sports and most of what I learned was positive for what I would do later in life. There were plenty of hard times and painful times, times I really regret. I know God had a plan through all of it and He wanted to teach me the lessons I needed to learn. By choosing not to play in college, I got to fully live. I served as a Residential Advisor, as staff on the Student Government Committee, President of several clubs, won Homecoming Queen my Sophomore year, ran for Student Body President my Senior Year, participated in a few college pageants, made countless friends, maintained almost a perfect grade-point average AND played intramural sports every season. I got to experience all this because I said no to what was safe to me. Continuing to play basketball would have been the safe choice. I knew it, I loved it and I could have succeeded at it. Letting it go and living new dreams was a risk. A risk I am so glad I took. When I got to play college sports at the intramural level, I got to really enjoy them, I got to laugh. Something I had not experienced in sports in many, many years. The joy for the game came back and I was playing at a high-level with a true love for it again. To this day, when I step back on a basketball court, I can still smell the fresh court lacquer. I can still feel all the feels of having a crowd cheer my name and the announcer saying my name across the intercom. I can feel the pain and I can feel the excitement. I can smile knowing the game brought me so much, but because I replaced the *hurt* of the game with the *joy*, I can walk onto a court now and smile.

I can always tell the ones who were athletes when I meet them later in life. They have this hunger, this drive, and they want to be coached. I call this "the athlete edge" and it's not something that can be taught, it's something that must be derived over years of trying and time.

Failing Publicly

When I was in college, I failed at several things. Public things. Things that should have totally embarrassed me. But I also won some major things too. I truly believe we become less resistant to failure the more we fail.

I ran for Student Body President and lost. I participated in the Miss University Pageant three times and lost. Those losses taught me so much. During the Student Government elections, I lost to an incumbent candidate who was also a friend. I lost by less than 10 votes. It might as well have been 100. After I picked myself off the floor and dried my tears, I realized I had two options. Stand up and serve my campus and be the best leader I could be, even if it meant I couldn't be the leader I wanted to be, or feel sorry for myself and watch from the sidelines. I chose option number 1. I took a seat on the President's Cabinet and led the Special Events Committee for the year. My leadership skills grew and I won Cabinet Member of the Year at the awards ceremony, I had a fantastic time. Fast forward many years later, I went on to sell the President and his new wife a new home and then another. Sometimes, when the future looks gloomy, it just means we have more learning to do. I know this for sure: If we do not say yes to God, we may never discover our strengths and learn to flourish. So, don't be afraid of the bad things that may happen. Be afraid of the things you could have said yes to and chose not to.

Someday we may be as grateful for the bad things as the good things, because the bad things helped prepare us for the good things. -Mark Batterson (In a Pit With A Lion On A Snowy Day, 82)

A 90% Failure Rate

I didn't know this business had a 90% failure rate. If I had, I probably wouldn't have started. Sometimes, what you don't know won't hurt you. I didn't know how likely I was to fail. In retrospect, that probably helped me succeed.

When I was 25 with a brand-new baby, I was let go from my salary-paying cushiony job. You want the truth? I hated that job. My favorite part of the day was when I got to go to the gym on my lunch hour and work out so that I could be around other people and interact! I was in the wrong profession with the wrong boss doing the wrong kind of work. My boss was rude, hateful and condescending. I literally dreaded going to work every day. The day I got let go from that job during a time of company layoffs and uncertainty, I was sad and scared, but I had my Real Estate License and I was eager. People told me when I started in Real Estate that it was a tough business. I heard it all. "You will run out of leads. Then what?" "Just get another safe job." You want to go from a salary job to 100% commission? That's crazy! That's such a risk."

Have you read the Bible lately? Faith is risk. Every notable character in the Bible is called to do something that requires great faith and they rise or fall due to their measure of faith. Sometimes God wants use to use our faith to step into places we cannot see, places so vast and scary that we think it may lead us into the valley. The truth is, God doesn't call us to do hard stuff, He calls us to do impossible stuff. And girlfriend, what you see as an impossible valley, God sees as your future mountaintop!

Faith is the substance of things hoped for. The evidence of things not seen.
Hebrews 11:1

The way I see it, there are two ways to view failures. We can see them as a way to give up and decide we are done. Or we can use them to inspire us to learn and keep going! No one is immune to failing. Even the greatest business owners, greatest athletes and most successful people on the planet have failed. Michael Jordan was one of my childhood heroes. Hey, I grew up in the 90s' when the Chicago Bulls were a big deal. I was the weird girl who had Michael Jordan posters in my room instead of Backstreet Boys. Don't get me wrong, I could jam out to "I Want It That Way" with all the other teenage girls. But I was more inspired by the likes of Michael, His Royal Airness. When someone plays at his caliber, we would expect a low level of failure, right? Wrong. Look at how many shots he missed. Look at how many times he failed. You know what? He picked himself up, practiced harder and kept taking the shots. And he went on to become unquestionably (at least in my mind), the greatest basketball player of all time. If he can do it, so can we.

As moms and business owners, we are so hard on ourselves. And that can be good! It drives us to be better, work harder and play until we slay! We also have to remember that losing is part of the process. Losing can teach us things that we could have never learned if we were constantly winning. Losing can change our mindset and make us take a different approach when needed.

Take Two

When I chose to re-brand my team, man, I was scared. I was afraid that people may think I had failed. I had several team members who had chosen to leave and go out on their own at that point, which is natural and normal in team environments. I internalized this pain of losing those women and internalized it into insecurity. I put on a brave face and tried to pretend I was okay but inside I felt like a failure. I was at a crossroads between re-building and quitting. I questioned my calling, my purpose for starting a team and my leadership abilities.

At that point, God put people in my life who spoke life into me. He gave me a supportive husband. He directed every message at church to speak right to my heart, as if it were written just for me. I realized that even though I felt like I had lost, I had grown in my leadership abilities. I had learned how to recruit the right kind of team members, I discovered that who I started with was not who I would end with and I became okay with that. I started fresh, I prayed for God's favor and guidance, I chose to believe in my abilities again and I went for it, really went for it.

"I could never be where I am now if I had stayed where I was back then", I said to my husband six months later. "Look at all that has happened in the last six months. Crazy, beautiful things that could never have happened if I would have stayed stuck in that bad environment, doubting myself and living as half of me." God allowed me to be broken in order to build me back up. And when He built me back up, He equipped me with strength and a passion that I had never known before. Thank the Lord for hard times that get us to the great times!

WHEN I LOSE
by Ashley

When I lose, I feel defeated. Because me, I like to
win.
When I lose, I feel insecure, that sinking feeling
washes over me again.
When I lose, I feel like giving up, like there is no need
trying again.
The truth is, when I lose, that is truly when I win.
Losing teaches us more than winning ever can.
It teaches us to rise above and how to make a future
plan.
Losing teaches us to prepare, work hard and grow
thick skin.
So that when we try again, we can face the next
challenge with a grin.
Losing teaches us to smile through the tears and let
the anger go.
Losing is the best way to help us really grow.
Losing is never fun, of this I can be sure.
But, in myself, it creates in me a resilience in
becoming secure.
Losing hurts and it may be painful for a while.
But in retrospect, I am happy to say it has come to
make me smile.
When I lose, I learn. I improve and I pray a ton.
I think back to the days of defeat and that is where I
won.

Discussion Questions:

Are there times you feel like you lost?

_____

_____

_____

_____

Looking back now, how have those times helped you?

_____

_____

_____

_____

Think about what you spent years pouring into
throughout your life. What did that time teach you?

_____

_____

_____

_____

Nobody Said It Was Easy

What Women Say: "The Mom-Guilt is so overwhelming. I never feel like I'm doing a good job. When I'm with my kids, I miss working. When I'm not working, I miss my kids. It's a constant battle."

What God Says: "God met me more than halfway, he freed me from my anxious fears." Psalm 34:4

"Have a tender heart but a tenacious spirit." - John Maxwell

Practical Tip: *Lay out your kids' clothes, backpacks and necessary items the night before you need them. Getting this done will save you time and stress the next morning as you're getting ready and trying to get everyone out the door.*

Goal of this Chapter: *The goal of this chapter is to help you eliminate excuses and focus on what's important. It will be truthful, direct and will point you on the path set before you so you can move forward in boldness.*

Countdown to Bedtime

"I'm so ready for bedtime" I tell my husband as he calls me on his way home from work. We chat during our normal routine time and talk about things from the day. "The kids did this, we went here and there, and I'm ready for supper, bath and bed". Maybe I can finally read the end of that book or catch up on a Netflix show, or most likely, work on my computer to finish up work stuff from the day. I just need to get to bed time, come on bedtime. I break up the 200th fight of the day and I sigh from the daily exhaustion. There are not many days that I'm not covered in baby slobber, dirt, markers and maybe some poop by the end. I always tell my husband I can't dress as well as him because the kids use me as a human dishrag. I am their shoulder to cry on, the shirt to wipe their messy hands on and everything seems to end up all over me each day. That's why a shower is required each night - to wash away all the germs, dirt and stuff from each day. When we lay the kids down each night (Glory!), I tell them I love them and we say prayers. I leave their room and think about how much I love them. When it's quiet and everyone is asleep, all I can think about is how much I love those little stinkers. Motherhood is weird, y'all.

It's All Mental

Have you ever run a long-distance race? If you have, you know how mental running can be. The physical aspect is important, of course, but I'm convinced that running is 80% mental. It's all about what you tell yourself, what you feed your mind and how determined you are to finish. Business and motherhood are a lot like that. Here is what I've learned: Tough situations don't last, tough people do. If you're determined to push through, do your best and aren't afraid to work really hard, then you're already 80% there. The other 20% will be put in through your actions. Your actions must follow your thoughts and words. You must have both to finish. Those who finish have both the skill and the determination.

No Sympathy

My husband says I have no sympathy. Before you think I'm too mean, he's referring to the times when he has a "man cold" and literally thinks he is dying. While he would prefer to be nurtured and coddled, I choose to ignore his pitiful pleas and keep on going. If this makes me mean, then so be it. I cannot handle his sad little condition and the way he cannot stand the thought of pressing through it. Bless my husband, he really is tough in every single way and strong and brave, but when it comes to needles and colds, he is a bowl full of Jell-O (Which I will never bring him when he is sick. Sorry, Babe.).

With this lack of sympathy, I find that it also translates into other areas of my life. I don't like excuses, laziness, flakiness or lies. If someone presents these things, I get frustrated. I think it's because my Momma raised me to: work really hard, do what you say you're gonna do, always tell the truth and fight for what you want! So, if I'm harsh in my words, please know that I come from a place of love, but I need to speak the truth into you as I write because I want you to know what it takes to be successful in your life.

But It's So Hard

Congratulations! You have chosen one of the most difficult professions, being a Momma and being a working Mom. Sometimes it feels like you're going crazy, or everything is going crazy, because your kids are crazy and your clients are acting crazy and you'll question yourself. Let me tell you this: It's not supposed to be easy.

"It's supposed to be hard. If it wasn't hard, everyone would do it. The hard...is what makes it great." - Jimmy Dugan, A League of Their Own

That quote is from one of my favorite sports movies. It comes during a time when the star of the team, the catcher, Dottie, wants to quit. Her jealous sister is mad at her and she is questioning her abilities and her desire to play. Her coach offered her this advice and convinced her to suit up for one more game, the final game.

Maybe it's hard right now because the hours are long. Maybe the nights are long (with a new baby or sick child). Maybe the balancing gets exhausting. Maybe your kids' school keeps getting canceled due to snow days and you really need to get in some work time. That happens too often. Breathe and realize that you've come to the right place. It was never supposed to be easy. When it's not easy, you know you've come to the right place.

Momma Needs An Extra Hour

While writing this book, I had to examine when I had an extra hour each time that I could focus on writing. I did not have any time to work on it during the day. My work and my kids took up all my waking hours. I could get up earlier but was already sleep-deprived due to a new baby under one and a toddler who loves to wake up screaming "Momma!!!!" at 2:00 and 4:00 a.m. every night for no apparent reason. So, the solution was this- work from 10:00 - 11:00 p.m. each night when the rest of the house was in bed. It wasn't a glamorous solution or one that was desirable, but it did make sense and it worked best for me! During that time, I was going to bed at midnight, being awoken by the baby at 2:00 and 5:00 a.m. to feed and care for. And then being awoken by my kids at 7:00 to start the day of motherhood and work! Those were long, tiring days but I saw the light at the end of the tunnel. Soon, the writing would be done. Soon, the baby would be sleeping through the night. I just had to focus and push through in order to get what I really wanted.

The point of this is - we must do what it takes to accomplish our goals. It may be waking up an hour earlier, working a few hours on the weekends, or staying up until midnight each night. If your goal is important enough to you, you'll find a way to make it happen!

The truth is- balancing mom life while being a mom boss usually isn't pretty. The good news is- it doesn't have to be! Sometimes it will be messy. Sometimes it means Chick-Fil-A drive through (Thank ya, Jesus!) between appointments while your kids are in the backseat. Sometimes it means locking yourself in the bathroom to take a phone call while your kids pound on the door needing you to open yet another juice box. Here's the BIG KEY- If you will keep your drive and have your goals and your why in front of you- you can be successful in both. You can be a Rockstar Momma and kill it in business. And you know what? You can do it with serving Jesus and living with integrity. I fully believe that, and I will confess it proudly!

Keep Your Foot on the Gas

I'm going to say it right now, and it's not going to make me very popular. But, it's the truth, and you need to hear it. You must not take your foot off the gas. Cruise control does not exist in motherhood or in running a business. You have to keep going and not stop learning, growing and getting better every day. If that scares you, then good, you've come to the right place. It doesn't have to be pretty. It doesn't even have to be neat. The truth is- sometimes it will be messy. But, if you keep your drive and have your goals in front of you- you can conquer them, both in motherhood and in business. It's a balancing act and it's about finding a rhythm. That rhythm can change by season. It can ebb and flow based on your family's needs and your goals for this particular season. But you cannot take your foot off the gas. You must create designated work days. Hear me on this, Momma. You must create designated work days. For me, that meant utilizing a Mother's Day Out Program for my kids starting at six months old. This was two days a week and it was local and at a church- several churches over the years- that I fully trusted. When MDO wasn't available, I scheduled a sitter during those days. Without fail- even on breaks and during the summertime. I kept my foot on the gas so the car would stay on course. When you take your foot off, you can start going slow, even get off-course. You can get too comfortable and go on cruise control. Don't use the brake pedal. Don't use the cruise control. Use the gas pedal and keep your plan in place. Your business depends on it. Enroll in the program, get a sitter and don't slack off. Your business is counting on you to be consistent. And when you're not, not only does it not propel you forward, it takes you backward! Keep your foot on the gas so the car will stay on course. Pick your work days, make arrangements and get to work! When you do this, you will have those non-work days to spend with your kids and enjoy days at home, days at the park and outings as a family. I love those days! I also love my work days. They bring me joy. Be diligent and create the life you want to have. This will only happen by putting in the work, girl. Do it, now.

The Power of Saying No

I get asked how I get all my work done with everything it takes it my industry. There are always things pulling me in every direction, if I would let them. An invite to this event, a class here, lunch with this group, appointments with clients, inspections and closings, and the list goes on. I could say yes to everything. But instead, I say no to most things. I work on my designated work days. I don't put things on my calendar on the days I'm not designated to work. Yes, I will still take phone calls, answer emails and do my necessary tasks. But I will not accept invites to luncheons, events and classes on those days. When I set up my days, I decided where I can say yes and where I will say no. Take charge, lay claim and don't look back. Learn to balance your life by taking care of your heart instead of just your calendar.

You know what else I say no to? The crazy number of kids' activities, birthday parties and events. Let me explain. With kids come all kinds of superfluous activities. It seems that everyone wants a piece of our child's time which means a piece of our family time. My husband and I decided a few years ago that there were certain things we would always say no to:

Classmate birthday parties: If our kids have 15 students in their class and each of them sends an invite to their birthday party, that means all our Saturdays would be filled up with birthday parties. We just say no. "No, thank you" to be polite. We refuse to allow these parties to eat up our family time when we could be using our time more wisely and effectively, like enjoying a family camping trip, going on a bike ride or hosting another family for a cookout.

My Kids' Activities: Y'all, please don't hate me. I love sports so much. But the kids' sports arena has gotten ridiculous. Games every weekend, practice twice a week and tournaments on Sundays. It's so consuming! We chose not to let our kids play on any sports events thus far and I don't see them starting in the near future. We have played in a six-week soccer league that meets in the fall and the spring and plays/practices on Saturday mornings only. The beauty of this is that it's a short season and it only takes up about two hours each Saturday. I also say yes to swim lessons for a week each summer. Other than that, right now, it's a no. I will not commit my kids and our family to all the crazy schedules out there. When they get older, yes, we will play sports. We are former athletes, after all. However, while they are young and we are the drivers, caretakers and plan makers, I will say no to all the time-consuming activities. I will say yes to: family dinners each evening around the table, yes to family walks each evening in the warm sunshine, yes to talking and playing and campouts together.

My Kids' Birthday Parties: I had to learn this one the hard way. When you have multiple children, the birthdays and the gifts really pile up. I used to throw Pinterest-worthy parties complete with all the party favors, pinata, birthday cake and matching plates. You know what I learned? My kids didn't care about the fancy party. The guests were still not happy with the food. The gifts were too much. I was stressed and tired. I said NO MORE. I said no to spending too much on the party, no to the stress and no the desire to please everyone. Now, we have "birthday experiences" where we choose a fun outing for the child with the birthday. We have gone on campouts with a bonfire and outdoor hiking, we have gone to a pumpkin patch and family farm and we have traveled for a great dinner and swimming in a hotel pool. The kids have loved it and they actually remember those special times! I invite our parents and grandparents over for dinner on their birthday and make an easy supper and a homemade birthday cake and we sing Happy Birthday to the happiest birthday kid ever! By saying no to structured parties, I said yes to: Family memories, no stress and a happy Momma and child.

Embracing the Chaos

My son threw up in my hand during an office meeting one time. Literally, threw up in my hand. I had to take him to work with me because he was sick and couldn't go to his school but acting fine and just clingy and cranky. He was two at the time and still very much needing Mommy. I held him during the office meeting where I talked about prospecting and planning. I was on a roll. "I got this", I thought. "I can rock this baby in my lap during a meeting thing". And then God laughed. My child started to vomit, and in true mom fashion, I stuck my hand out to catch it mid-air before it hit the floor. I carried the said vomit to the trash can, threw it away, wiped down my child and changed his shirt. And then I gave him a drink of water, held him tight and finished the meeting. That's embracing the chaos 101.

If there is one thing I can tell you to help you enjoy your life and become more productive while being a mom, it's this: embrace the stinkin' chaos. It's not going away, sister. Kids are wild and they are loud and they need you. All the time. Especially when you're trying to go potty in peace for two minutes. I guarantee you that someone will need something from you right that very moment. We cannot get rid of the chaos that it raising kids. But here's how I see it. We can either let it drive us crazy and cripple our ability to be effective OR we can embrace this season of our lives and make the best of it. So, laugh when things aren't pretty, laugh when it's loud and chaotic and your kids are fighting for the tenth time today, laugh when you have to take your child to work with you because he's sick but you must give that presentation. It's going to happen. I promise you, it will. But choose your response carefully and know that this season too, will pass.

Right now, right this second, you must decide to stop being a helicopter mom. You must embrace the chaos. Or you will drown in it.

If you were to stop by my house during the week at say 2:00 p.m., you would laugh at what my day looks like. Some may call it controlled chaos, but hey- my circus, my monkeys! My kids would be playing and having fun, my house would be mostly clean and I would be doing something productive, whether that would be writing, cooking, cleaning or working on a contract. Productive can mean a lot of things and whatever it means for you, own it. Create the life you want through embracing the chaos and living productive days which equate to a productive life!

Mom Truths
By Ashley

I've had a natural birth. I've had an epidural.

I've breastfed extensively. I've pumped exclusively.

I've made my own baby food. I've let my baby eat french fries.

I've cloth diapered. I've used thousands of disposable diapers.

I've made my kids home-cooked breakfast meals. I've given my kids processed foods that come in bags for breakfast as we race out the door.

I've arranged full days of playtime and outside fun. I've let my kids watch way too much tv.

I've blended my kids into my business flawlessly. I've locked my kids in the house to escape the craziness while I run on the front porch to talk to a client on the phone for a few minutes.

I've laughed while my kids get muddy and play. I've gotten frustrated at my kids for spilling their milk.

I've succeeded. I've messed up. I've triumphed. I've failed. Through it all, God uses my weaknesses for His glory.

Be authentic. Perfectionism is overrated.

Discussion Questions:

How can you keep your foot on the gas in this upcoming season?

_____

_____

_____

_____

What days will you make your designated work days?

_____

_____

_____

_____

What will you say no to that's taking up too much of your time?

_____

_____

_____

_____

MOMMIN' With Courage

What Women Say: "Some people don't understand why I want a large family, how I discipline my children and the choices my husband and I make for our family."

What God Says: "Don't you see that children are God's best gift? The fruit of the womb his generous legacy? Like a warrior's fistful of arrows are the children of a vigorous youth. Oh, how blessed are you parents, with your quivers full of children!" Psalm 127:3 (MSG)

"When you desire your dreams more than your comfort, you'll do whatever it takes to make it happen." – Pastor Lisa Kai

Practical Tip: *Our children have their own separate goals list. They get to decide what their goals are for the semester at school. When the semester starts, this goal seems huge and unattainable. As we get into the middle, they start to see the light at the end. And then at the end, they achieve it. We allow them to choose what they want for their goal prize and use this as an incentive to reach for their goals, even during times when they want to quit. It's important to start implementing these practices young!*

Goal of this Chapter: *The Goal of this chapter is truly to show you that it's okay to love what you do! It's okay to love working while being a mom. We can do both! These chapter includes wisdom on how to do both and do them even better!*

Standing Firm

Having children, raising children- it's something each parent must decide on and stand firm on, against what others think. Family and friends may not understand the many choices that we must make for our children: The number we choose to have, vaccinating vs. not vaccinating, daycare vs. stay-at-home. It seems that everyone wants to have an opinion on how we raise our families. If you're not confident in yourself, in your choices and in God's calling, you can easily be swayed by the world's voices. I've done my own thing and carved a path that was different than what others may have envisioned. That's not to say that my choices did not come with their own hurts and effects. People may say things to you that make you question your choices and convictions but it's your choice to stay strong, be bold in your decision making as you and your spouse plan your life together, with God at the center of it all.

But I Love To Work

I love going to work. I love going into the office. I love going on appointments. Sometimes, it's more exciting, fulfilling and easy to go to work rather than spend the day with my children. Wait, did I just say that out loud? Yes, I believe I did. Man, parenting is draining and exhausting at times. At work, I can control so much more than I can around my toddler who bursts into tears at the drop of a hat. Literally. I am fully convinced that God gave us toddlers to develop our patience. I know mine sure does. The sad part is, as women, we feel guilty when we love our work, when we enjoy doing our jobs, when we go on date nights with our husband. I know I do! Why do we do this to ourselves? I know this is true - God made you to fulfill a specific calling for such a time as this. I refuse to let the mom guilt over-shadow my calling. I love my work and I love my kids. I will embrace both and not let shame come into my heart and mind. Not today, Satan. Not today.

The Downfall of Excuses

When people ask me, "how do you do it all"? Here is my number one answer: I don't and I can't. I am not perfect, nor do I have it all figured out. I ask for help and hire help when needed. I am intentional. I am intentional with my time, with my schedule and with what I want our future to look like. I often coach women to imagine their lives five years down the road. Really allow themselves to dream and then imagine five years down the road. Now, work backwards. What steps must be taken today in order to make those dreams a reality in five years? Building a career, having a family, buying a new home - those dreams can all begin today.

Momma, here's the deal. We have to quit making excuses. Excuses are the biggest deterrent to our success. I see it so often. A woman comes to me and tells me she wants to be successful, have a great career, be a high producer, etc. But when I ask her about her daily habits and structure, she has none. And then there come the excuses of why she hasn't done the things she wants to do. All I hear is excuses. Some of them are logical and even accurate, but none of them are unattainable.

Whether it's school drop off lines, laundry, lack of time or something else, anything can be overcome with a little planning and a strong desire to succeed.

I think it's important that we plan our days before they happen. Plan our weeks before they come. Have a plan. That doesn't mean your plan will play out perfectly, but at least you will have an end goal in mind. Be the successful woman you see yourself as in five years. That starts today.

The Power of Delegating

"Only do what only you can do." I heard these words spoken by Pastor Craig Groeschel and they truly changed my mindset. I started making a list of things only I could do at work and at home. When I did this, I gained perspective and I gained more time for what I needed to do. I delegated the tasks at work that I could "give away". But there were some things I need to do because I do them best. Sometimes, it's hard to give things away because we don't want to trust another person to do something we take so much pride in. If we communicate our needs, set expectations and train well, these tasks CAN be given away.

I am a very hands-on mom. I want to do everything for my family. I want to be the one to handle our schedule, our groceries, our home. But, when I had too many irons in the fire, I decided it was time to get some help at home and give some tasks away, especially during those busy seasons. Here are some examples of things you can give away: Home cleaning, grocery shopping, yard work, laundry, car washing and interior cleaning, even cleaning! If it doesn't bring you joy and causes frustration and worry constantly, just give it away. Find a way, make a way, create a way.

You may need to give something away but you're holding back for some reason. Giving things away can give you back your time and help you be your best!

Raising Quality Kids

I'm still in the raising stage of motherhood. Perhaps I'll write a book one day when my children are grown about how I did it, how wonderful my children are and how train your children into becoming wonderful adults. I'm not there yet and I don't claim to be an expert in this area. I do know that creating quality time and experiences for our children is a big priority to my husband and I. We do this by making sure our children learn the value of hard work, have their own responsibilities and have a schedule they can rely on.

Hard work- In order to instill hard work, our children first witness their parents working hard. They see that work is not something we must do, but something we get to do! When they see their parents enjoying their work and finding joy in what we do, they see that work is valuable and something to look forward to and not dread. We also take our children with us when we work outside in the front yard, cutting down tree limbs, landscaping, taking care of our goats and cleaning inside. They learn that everything has a purpose and the care of making those things look nice belongs to us to get things done.

Responsibilities - It's important for kids to have their own responsibilities, whether it be chores or different tasks that belong solely to them. As my kids get older and are able to do more, I'll be able to give them more tasks to do. Right now, my kids must make their own beds, clean up their own playroom and help take care of our animals. This gives them a sense of keeping things clean and taking pride in their work. The kids enjoy taking care of our goats by watering and feeding them, caring for the baby goats after they are born and cleaning out their barn when needed. We also have a dog and they can help with feeding, bathing and all other dog duties that may be needed. Responsibilities do not limit children, they empower them.

Schedule - Children flourish with boundaries and security. Creating a set bedtime is something small that can create a schedule for them. During the winter months, when it's dark so early, our bedtime is 8:00 p.m. During the Summer and warmer months, we focus on spending more time outdoors and bedtime can get pushed back to 8:45-9:00. Whatever the bedtime may be, you must be intentional and stern about it. Our children also know what each day means. They know that Sundays mean church which is non-negotiable. Week days mean school days. Each day has a meaning and a purpose and they look forward to what each day with bring. Another non-negotiable for our family is meal time. Mealtime happens every evening around our dining room table. We pray, eat together and talk and then we clear the table and clean up after the meal. This is a set time when we know we will all be together and it's always spent with no television or distractions. Establishing routines and schedules provides security and confidence.

CHAOS!

Your Best Is The Best

For all your moms out there wondering if you're doing enough for your kids. All the single mommas, divorced, hard-working women who are trying to provide yet still get dinner on the table every night, you are awesome. You are doing your best and your kids will see that. When we worry about our kids' perception and what their memories will be, I know it's tough to see it now. Make sure your kids see how much you love them and spend that quality time together. Make the moments count. Let go of the mom guilt and remember, God gave your children to you because you are the best mom for them! They will look back and remember the time you spent with them. They will look back and smile. You just need to embrace your season and love them. Just remember that your situation does not have to define you. Whatever season you're in, use that season to give you a passion. That passion may very well lead to your platform. I've known single moms that would out work anyone else in the room. This is because they chose to let go of excuses and do something great to support their family. I've also known parents of special needs children who have every excuse in the world to sit home and cry. Instead, they chose not to feel sorry for themselves and built a platform around their "place in life" to inspire others. This is how we become our best! Look for those examples all around you and let them encourage you to get rid of the excuses and start creating the life you desire, girlfriend!

Someday, it will be worth it.
By Ashley

Changing another diaper, for the 100th time it seems. I long for a time far off when there are no more clean-ups but that's only in my dreams.

Someday, it will be worth it, all this time spent changing diapers, feeding the baby and getting up all night. Someday, it will be worth it.

The kids are fighting in the car. I am about to lose my mind. Their constant bickering and arguing really puts me in a bind.

Someday it will be worth it, all this refereeing fights, correcting bad behavior and discipling these children to be kind. Someday it will be worth it.

Making school lunches every day, it's really such a chore. Packing their bags and cleaning their messes, it can really be a chore.

Someday, it will be worth it. My kids will pack for each day for themselves. They can choose their own clothes, clean up their own floors and won't need me for everything anymore. Someday, it will be worth it.

Maybe the someday I have been longing for is meant to be fully lived today.

Maybe God uses these little moments to teach us grace along the way.

Maybe the tasks of motherhood are extraordinary after all.

Maybe the mission of motherhood is part of our Heavenly call.

Discussion Questions:

What guilt can you let go of today?

_____

_____

_____

_____

What can you give away at work and at home?

work: stories, uploading mealplans

home: groceries, cleaning, cooking?

How can you ensure that you are raising quality kids?

1. solid bed time
2. All start @ 7: books/ prayers, twins real bed @ 8:15
3. responsibilities
4 grateful!

Living Authentically

What Women Say: "I am often intimidated by everything and everyone who relies on me every day. I don't know how to make everyone happy."

What God Says: Be strong. Take courage. Don't be intimidated. Don't give them a second thought because God, your God, is striding ahead of you. He's right there with you. He won't let you down; he won't leave you." Deuteronomy 31:6

> *"Don't like a compartmentalized life. Live an interconnected life." - Cristine Caine (The Messy Table Podcast)*

Practical Tip: *Get on the same page with your spouse. If you want to create a solid marriage, communication is key. Hold meetings together where you can plan out your family goals and establish plans to put into place. Be excited and work toward these things together. And here is an intimate tip: if you're married and live together, shower together. That's been a secret of ours for a long while.*

The Goal of This Chapter: *The goal of this chapter is to give you the confidence to live fully and freely. Living authentically is the best and only way to truly live in freedom. You will be able to focus on what your calling is and how you can make sure you are living to achieve it.*

Baby, Bye, Bye, Bye

I don't know about you but every time I read this title, my mind goes back to the year 2000. N'Sync takes the stage and we hear the "hey, hey" ... "Baby, Bye, Bye, Bye". Come on now, I can't be the only one! That brings back some memories right there! If you're too young to recall the glorious N'SYNC days, I'm sorry, please bear with me. I thought this was a catchy title. It's also a good thing to say to negativity. That includes negative thoughts, actions and people. Bye, bye, bye.

You know, the older I get, the more I realize that you gotta tell some things goodbye. Things that aren't good for you, things that aren't growing you and things that just aren't right for you. God called us to live upright, holy and boldly. We have our strength, courage and His power to accomplish our callings. Why do we waste our time being tied down to things that bring us down? Let's dive right into this. Stay with me, girl. You're not gonna want to miss this one.

Bye, Bye to the 9-5

I knew as soon as I had my first child that I wanted to be home with my kids most of the day but I knew I was called to work and not be home full-time. The solution that worked for me from the beginning was to find a Mother's Day Out Program. My kids have gone. to several different ones throughout the years, depending on where we were living at the time and their ages. These programs have allowed my children to go to their classes 2 days week and gain social skills, learning, get playtime and have lunches and naps alongside their peers. These have all been faith-based as they have been inside churches so they also get to learn about the Lord, read Bible verses and make crafts with biblical references. It's absolutely fantastic! These two days per week have given me about 10 hours per week that I can focus on my business. I am able to do all the work I need to do during these two days which includes office time, time for work and personal appointments, business planning, lunch dates, etc. When I need to work additional hours, I make those times on the weekend when their daddy can help. There are always circumstances when they are out of school for a holiday or when an appointment falls on a day when they are out of school. In these circumstances, I try to have at least one babysitter on call that can come over for a few hours. Summertime is always a bit of a challenge too with this structure but I have been able to work around it by adjusting my schedule, finding a summertime program that offers 1-2 day per week sessions and I bring a babysitter to help out one day per week as well. The month of August is usually entirely free and then programs take off. So, I plan to spend more time with my kids during this time, we vacation, and I plan extra activities for us to have fun and finish off summer strong! This has worked so well for my schedule. I am able to work and feel like a 100% mom which is what I really wanted. I know I am blessed that this has worked so well for me.

I saw a life where I could drop off my kids to school and pick them up. I saw a life where I could work a fulfilling job where I helped people and made a difference. I saw being able to keep a clean home, have dinner on the table each night for my family, host family and friends at our home for gatherings, attend church together as a family each Sunday and spend plenty of quality time. I wanted a career that allowed me to make an income to help support our family and allowed us to live and give in a way that we could be proud of. When we made our vision board, we pictured being able to tithe greatly to our local Church, travel when we desired, live in a home that made us happy and secure and raise our children in an excellent environment. That is why I wanted a 100% life, 100% at home and 100% at work.

Bloom

My perspective has changed a lot since starting my business. As you can imagine, I have learned, grown and developed over the years. My perspective has changed. And, girlfriend, yours will too. The important thing is that you must get out there and live! I wish I could teach you all I have learned and prevent you from making the mistakes I have made, guard you from the pain I have felt. But then you wouldn't grow in the way you are supposed to and you wouldn't bloom at the right time". *The Bible says "So the Master, God, brings righteousness into full bloom and puts praise on display before the nations. (Isaiah 61:10).* A flower cannot bloom until it's ready. Until it's been watered, the sun has beat down on it, and its petals cannot stand being pinned up any longer. That will be you. Sometimes we are being watered and feel like we are flourishing, sometimes the sun is shining on us and we feel warm and toasty. Sometimes that dreaded sunshine becomes too hot, and we feel like we are going to burst due to the pressure. And then, we open up. We blossom. We shine beautifully. All in God's timing. Stay the course, girlfriend. Don't be afraid of the course the flower takes. That flower is you.

What Are You Called To Do?

Make a list of what you believe you are called to do, who you are called to be. Think hard, close your eyes and imagine. Really let yourself imagine what really fulfills you. Ask God to show you. Who are you deep down? Here is what I feel I am called to do:

> *Speak Life*
> *Encourage Others*
> *Lay hands on and pray*
> *Lead and be an example*
> *Be a light*
> *Help others achieve their goals*
> *Raise children who will be lights for the Lord*
> *Raise children who care about people*
> *Raise children who believe in doing what's right*
> *Raise children who are strong and kind*
> *Be fierce- in my life, in my marriage, career, and with my kids*
> *Be intentional- with all my relationships, with my time and with my future*

Not only are we called to speak life into others, we need life spoken into us as well. It's important to find ways to bring joyful words and encouragement into your own mind and heart. I find that these ways are all helpful to me: praying for God's favor, reading my Bible as well as a daily devotional, surrounding myself with Godly women as friends, listening to uplifting podcasts, reading inspiring books, following inspirational women on social media, not focusing on negative people, relationships or situations. If you want to speak life into others, you must have life spoken into you. Discover your ways.

Fearlessly Authentic

In our world of social media, selfies and the pressure for perfection, it's hard to know what's real, what's right and who you should be. I used to think I had to portray myself as perfect, as having it all together and as a Mom who never lets my kids wear me down. I have discovered that this is the furthest thing from the truth. People want you to show your real self. Here is what I have discovered, and Craig Groeschel says it best: "People would rather follow a leader who is always real than one who is always right."

So, don't be afraid to be yourself. You know the posts on my Facebook page that get the most likes? It's not my pretty professional pictures or posts about houses I have sold. The ones people like to see the most are those where things are a mess, when things are funny and things which they can relate! The best moments are when my kids say something, when they make a total mess or when they totally embarrass me in public!

I had one funny story in which people loved reading about. It was when I asked my kids what they wanted their new baby brother to be. I was about to do the gender-reveal ultrasound and we were so excited to find out if baby number four would be a girl or a boy! As we played outside, I asked my kids, "Do you want the new baby to be a brother or a sister?" Brylee, the oldest sweetly said "A sister! I want a sister!" I knew that's what she would say because she had been saying it for months. What I didn't expect was my oldest son's response. "Bowen, I asked, "what do you want the new baby to be?" And without hesitation, he answered, as serious as a three-year-old can be "I want him to be a LION!" I laughed and laughed. I didn't even know how to respond. I took a picture of my three kids playing outside and posted the it along with the story on Facebook later that day. It got so much attention. Not because I tried to make it sound like the perfect moment. But because I showcased it as it was, a real moment. People appreciate authenticity. They see through fakeness and you cannot hide a genuine spirit. I'm proud to say that the next day, we found out we were definitely not having a lion, but another perfect baby boy.

Showing funny things, sad things and hard things and yes, even amazingly happy things, make us real. They make us relatable. And by showing that we are real, we become authentic. You know, I encourage my team to be "fearlessly authentic" in their lives. That means, living with courage and working hard. Loving God and loving people. And realizing that we are all just working through the mess of life.

You know, having 4 kids and running a business while balancing all of life's duties is not easy. Are there some days I feel like tearing my hair out and wish I had less laundry, less messes, lower grocery bills and more "me" time? Yes. But this life is not about me. It's about joining hands with Jesus to fulfill whatever tasks He sets before me and to share His love with all He brings my way".

MOM PREP - A note to my pre-baby self.
By Ashley

Learn to love and live in elastic waistbands.

Get used to being up and down at all hours of the night and functioning on a few blinks each night. I don't know when this ends because I'm not there yet.

Be okay with wearing spit-up on the shoulders of your shirts.

Feel confident wearing nursing tops like you run the world.

Never expect to finish a full meal sitting at the table.

Live for nap time and bed time so you can have short segments of quiet.

Never be allowed to use the bathroom or shower alone…ever again. Their curious eyes will find you!

Become a nurse, maid, teacher, friend, chaperone, stylist, cook, referee and so many things you never knew you could be.

Get ready to experience your heart living outside your chest. Because it really, truly will.

Don't expect motherhood or anything else of great value to come easily.

Discussion Questions:

What do you feel called to do?

_____

_____

_____

_____

What can you say "bye, bye, bye" to that will help you move forward?

_____

_____

_____

_____

How can you live more authentically in your life?

_____

_____

_____

_____

Ashley Schubert

From Surviving to Thriving

What Women Say: "I know the life I want. I don't know how to take the first step to get it."

What God Says: God ALWAYS calls us to go FIRST.

"The difference between successful people and others is how long they spend time feeling sorry for themselves." - Barbara Corcoran

Practical Tip: *Say a prayer each morning as the first thing you do for the day. As soon as you wake up, pray. This will change your life, literally, and start your day off with confidence. Wake, Pray, Slay.*

Goal of this chapter: *The goal of this chapter is to show you that you have to go for it and create the life you want. I have to admit, I loved writing this chapter. These words I wrote made me feel bold. Please take them as encouragement as you stop making excuses and start building your dream life.*

Moving Past Mediocre

In order to do what other people don't do, you have to do the things that most people won't do. If you want to be average, just do what everyone else does. If you want to stand out, just step beyond average. I have made a list of things, in my profession, that the average person does. I then think about how I can take a step beyond and be better than average. If you want to be average in business, do these things:

- *Work only when you have an appointment.*
- *Skip meetings when you have a conflict.*
- *Only go to classes when you need credits.*
- *Say thank you with words only.*
- *Skip reading/podcasts/learning.*
- *Don't answer your phone or respond to texts.*

If you want to stand out and go beyond average, do these things:

- *Work consistently, even when there is nothing on your schedule.*
- *Attend all meetings and make them a priority.*
- *Make classes a necessity for growth and development.*
- *Say thank you with follow-up personal notes and tokens to show you care.*
- *Always be learning- read to grow.*
- *Answer your STINKIN' phone! Respond to text messages.*

These tips are as practical as it gets. Nothing complicated but definitely not common practice. Change these things about yourself and your business will change, improve and grow. If you want to move past mediocre, stop making average choices.

Getting Past Survival Mode

"What are your goals for this next year?" I ask women often. I hear so many women often say "I'm just trying to survive this week! There is no way I can put more on my plate." When I ask them what their plans are for their business this summer, I commonly get the answer "My kids will be out of school so I have to take care of them all the time. It will be hard to get any work done, I'll just be surviving". This is survival mode. And survival mode is a tough way to live. The good news is- you can get past survival mode. You can go from just surviving to fully thriving! It's going to take work, planning and sticking to your plans. There are five areas that will help:

- *Manage the Clutter*
- *Quit Making Excuses*
- *Build the Life You Want*
- *Super Intentional Time*
- *Creating Your Tribe*

Managing the Clutter

When my house is clean, I feel calmer. When my kids are happily playing outside, I feel proud and at peace. When I'm caught up on work, I feel productive. So why do we allow so much clutter into our lives?

I read a bible verse and my devotional this morning. It really struck a chord with me and I loved it. Here it is:

"She looks well to the ways of her household and does not eat the bread of idleness". Proverbs 31:27

Now I know the Proverbs 31 is a bit crazy and it seems she can do it all! I view her as an example of what we can strive to be. It's not that we have to strive for perfection, but for progress.

Living in achievement mode is what keeps me going. Achieving makes me feel empowered. The need to achieve is also my kryptonite. I think this can be useful however because I can help others tackle their achievements, and this brings me joy.

Sometimes it's just easier to think about doing things than actually doing them, right? Dreaming of the things we could do is easier than actually putting them into practice. It doesn't have to be.

I challenge you today to do one thing that you have been wanting to do. Cross something off your list that will make you feel proud. It's amazing what crossing something off your list will do for your mindset. So--- just do it! Clean out your closet. Decorate that wall that you already have a vision for in your mind. Get the laundry all caught up. Start somewhere. Ask for help. Get it done. You'll be glad you did.

Quit Making Excuses, Momma

"How many houses are you going to sell today, Momma?" My daughter asks this every time I go out the door for a work appointment. "I'm hoping for one, sweetie", I say with a laugh. Without missing a beat, she replies "I think you should sell three". Alrighty, then. My daughter doesn't understand that it's not possible to sell three houses in that one day. She doesn't know that it's not going to happen. For her, if you can sell one then you can surely sell three.

Sometimes, we sell ourselves short. We let excuses get in the way of what we can really accomplish.

I'm a very "get it done" type of person. I'm not a perfectionist. That's definitely a downfall of mine. It drives my husband crazy. I can often be found with a tag still hanging off my new dress because I didn't notice it or with my bra strap twisted because I didn't bother to worry about it. I used to drive my mom crazy with these things too. I just naturally don't sweat the small stuff. But, hey, because of this, I can get a lot done and can accomplish a lot in a short time. When it comes to getting things done, I always say "just do it". You don't have to know why, or even necessarily how, but just know that you must start somewhere. You must take the first step. Don't worry about things being perfect, worry about never making the choice to step out in faith.

Build It Up, Girl

My team was about four years in the making when I realized we need to make some changes. I needed to change things and create a re-brand if this team was really going to grow and excel in the future.

What do you want your brand to say about you? What do you want people to think about when they see your name or business name? Sit down and write these words out. Write a mission statement, a vision statement and even what an ideal team member or client would look like. When I re-branded my team at the end of 2018, it was scary and uncertain. I even had my brokers tell me not to do it, it wasn't safe. After praying about it and knowing in my heart it was the right move, I made the call. We were changing the name of my team to reflect the direction in which we were headed to create the future we needed. I want to give you a peek into our new team member packets. Here is some of the language I included to cast the vision:

Mission: Creating Excellence, Influence and Prosperity

Team Atmosphere Goal: To grow in a vigorous way as a result of a favorable environment.

Expectations: This is a place to grow, develop and become better together. As a group of women, we will help each other become better. We will succeed as we strive to reach a common goal. We will flourish in business, home and in life!

By laying it out there and showing the women what it looked like to be on the team, it put us all on the same page. Expectations were set and they knew the desired atmosphere that we sought. By doing this, it ensured all the women were of the same mindset and wanted to be team players. I always say that I hire based on quality, rather than hiring just to growing the quantity of team members. I want to grow my team the right way, not by stacking numbers, but by creating a solid group of women.

Super Intentional Time

I'm not very good at sitting. Some people may see this as a blessing and usually it is. My number one strength on the Gallup Strengths finder Test is "Achiever" followed by "Competitor" and "Woo" (Winning Others Over). Yikes. These are amazingly strong strengths, especially for what I do. However, they can be a real thorn in my side. If I'm not achieving something, I feel lazy, bad about myself and just off. Even if it's organizing a closet while I'm at home, I need something to keep me busy and give me a task to check off my list. This drives my husband crazy about me but he knows this just who I am. I am not good at rest, not good at sick days and not good at time off. I would rather be working, doing and accomplishing something. I have to make myself sit down and rest, make myself take days off or vacations. I feel guilty when I'm not working or doing something of value. When people ask me how I get so much done, I think this is why. I am wired as an achiever. For some reason, God wanted to make me this way. I'm working on making myself rest sometimes because rest can be a very good thing to restore our mind, body and reset our vision. Like everything else, there must be a balance between work and rest. If you rest too much, you become a sluggard. If you work yourself too hard, your mind and body don't respond well, and you will suffer the consequences of burnout. I can feel burnout when it's coming on and I've learned to take a few days bringing happiness in and letting stress out. For me, that entails praying and reading scripture, being outside and walking, soaking up the sunshine, writing and being with my family. Those things restore me. What restores you? You need to know so you can push that RESET button when needed.

When you only have 10 hours per week to work on your business, you take it seriously. My kiddos were only in their program for a few hours per week, so I had to learn how to make the most of this time. I learned quickly that using a day planner is the only way to live effectively. If you don't have one, get one immediately. Start writing down your appointments, goals, and everything you plan to do each month. Go over it weekly, plan your week before it happens and you'll be amazed at how much you can accomplish!

"It's not how much time you spend, it's how you spend your time." -Brian Buffini

This year has been full of growth for me. I finally get it. I'm in my 30s, ya'll...and I finally get it! Life is all about living intentionally. It's NOT waking up each day to discover what's going to happen to us, it's NOT doing our best when the opportunities present themselves, it's NOT about letting life "happen to us". It's about making the most out of our time and LIVING ON PURPOSE.

We all have the same amount of time in each day. 24 hours. How we prioritize that time is up to us. As moms, we dedicate so much of that time to our children. And that's as it should be. When we own a business, that business is our "baby" and takes a lot of time and nurturing as well. Many days, the 24 hours we are given is not enough. But we must make it count. Here are the ways I make sure my time is being spent well:

- I live by my daily planner. I prefer to write things down in an old school planner versus the calendar on my iPhone. Writing helps put things in my memory bank. When I write things down, I remember them. I can also cross things off, make notes in the margin, etc.
- Make to-do lists. Make these daily, weekly and monthly. Cross items off as you do them. It's also wise to make a "master to-do list" of things you want to accomplish and mark them off as they are completed. By the way, is there any greater feeling than crossing things off a to-do list? Can I get an Amen?!
- Create checkpoints along the way. If you have a major goal to accomplish, it's good to break it up into small checkpoints along the way. If you want to complete a task during a season, break

it up into smaller lots and set small goals along the way. The feeling of accomplishment will help as you complete each goal, it will make the big goal seem doable and before you know it, you will have slayed the big goal.

- Plan your day before the day begins, your week before the week begins and your month before the month begins. This will help you stay on course and not get swayed by small inconveniences and distractions.
- As always, begin and end each day with prayer. You will be amazed how much this will help your spiritual journey as well as your overall life.

Do one thing every day

This is so important when you have a long-term goal in mind for your business, your family or both! Even though you cannot do it ALL every day. You can do a little bit every day, every single day. If you are trying to grow your business, set a goal to make 5 new contacts every day, write 5 note cards or 5 make phone calls. If you are trying to spend more quality time with your children, read one book per day, sing 3 songs together each day or spend 20 minutes outside together. All the little things will add up to become BIG THINGS.

The key to all of this is to LIVE INTENTIONALLY. Have a purpose behind why you do what you do. When you discover the value to intentional living, that's when your BEST LIFE can begin.

I like to write a list of everything I need to accomplish and then give each item a deadline. For instance, when I was writing this book, I had to lay out each thing that needed to be done and when it needed to be done. There was a first draft date, a second draft date and a book deadline. A front cover design deadline, an editing deadline and a final deadline to send it in. There were marketing timelines and launch team prospecting, book signing deal dates and so much more. A lot goes into writing a book, that's for sure! When I looked at the big picture of everything that needed to be accomplished it was scary and overwhelming. When I broke it down into pieces and separated everything out, it became much more attainable and I could move forward in confidence. As they say "The best way to eat an elephant is one bite at a time".

Creating Your Tribe

Do you remember what it was like when you were a kid, performing or playing sports? You were in front of people often and you had an audience. If you played basketball or softball like me, you had people cheering for you in the stands. There were always supporters, always encouragers, always fans. And then you grew up, you got married, got a girl career and realized that your fans were no longer there. It all happened so quickly. You wonder "where did they go"? Do I have anyone in my corner anymore. You do, sister. You just have to look more diligently than you did when you were 16. You have to actually work to establish a tribe. You have to create the life you want to have. If you husband and children, then you already have people who admire you more than life itself. Be the you that they see in you. Do you have a church group or a women's group you are a part of? I hope so. If not, I encourage you to get one or even start one. This little circle can change your life. Do you have a mom group who can swap stories and share tips and help? Find that. Find ways to plug in and be intentional about it. If you are in a business where you have clients, utilize these relationships and ask for reviews and testimonials. And don't forget to treat these people well. Your cheering section is still out there. It just won't come naturally anymore. You must selectively bring it together.

It's so true that as women, we are fueled by the people we surround ourselves with. Whether that be family, friends or work associates, we become who we hang out with. As Pastor Craig Groeschel says, *"Show me your friends and I will show you your future"*.

I have such a passion for inspiring other women to live their best lives! That can only be done when we first change our "circle" to ensure we are surrounded by positive individuals. I'm not saying we can't have friends who are on the negative side or that we can't take a friend out for coffee who is down in the dumps. In fact, it's necessary to sow into other people who need encouragement! It becomes a downfall when you allow these people to influence your behavior and attitude. That happens when we spend too much time in negative situations with negative personalities. Jesus calls us to be "a light unto the World" and we should be! If we don't showcase his light, who will? But, in order to be equipped to do this, we must be surrounded by individuals who motivate, inspire and cause us to be the best versions of ourselves.

In order to do this, we need to periodically evaluate our friend list. It's okay to distance yourself from friends who don't fit well into---you becoming a better YOU! Never, ever burn bridges but put a space in there if necessary, through prayer and following God's leading.

Remember this: *"Your vibe attracts your tribe"*. I find so much truth in this! When you're positive, you attract positive people. That's just the way it is. When you have a good outlook on life, are happy and wear a smile, like-minded individuals will surface and be added into your circle.

Look for ways to compliment other women. As females, we need compliments every now and then! Tell a friend or even a stranger that you like her outfit, her hair, etc. And be genuine when you say it! This can make a world of difference in someone's day. And when we bless others, we in turn, are blessed.

I am so honored to be surrounded by wonderful women on my Real Estate team. They are all positive, Christian ladies working toward a common goal and I honestly could not be prouder to call them my tribe. I also have several friend groups including my bible study group, real estate friends and friends with kiddos. I make it a point to spend time with each of these groups in order to build relationships and cultivate growth and trust.

Another way we can surround ourselves with positive influences is by reading and listening to good content. Whether that be Christian radio, an upbeat podcast or a great book, these are all avenues to lift our spirits. I love reading books about other female entrepreneurs who have achieved success. I can learn from them and cast a vision for my future. I also love a good podcast when I'm driving. They allow me to zone in, focus and listen to some helpful content. Fill your mind with things that matter!

Be your best, surround yourself with positivity and pour into others. When you feel inspired, you will most definitely be the best YOU.

I Believe
By Ashley

I believe strongly in the power of prayer and hard work.

I believe in treating others well and being kind.

I believe that a home should be life-giving with open doors and plenty of seats at the dinner table.

I believe that marriage should be forever and love should keep growing continually.

I believe that children should get dirty and playing outdoors should be a requirement.

I believe that everyone we meet has a story and a purpose.

I believe that we are all on a journey and only God can determine our final destination.

Discussion Questions:

In what way are you just surviving right now?

_____

_____

_____

_____

What can you do to ensure your days are productive?

_____

_____

_____

_____

What kind of tribe can you create that will help make you better and that you can pour into?

_____

_____

_____

_____

Fearlessly Forward

What Women Say: "I struggle with multi-tasking and organization."

What God Says: "Refuse good advice and watch your plans fail; take good counsel and watch them succeed." Proverbs 15:22 (MSG)

"There are three questions someone will ask before working with you. Can I trust you? Are you good at what you do? Do you care about me?" - Lou Holtz

Practical Tip: *Schedule time to spend with your spouse. Schedule time to spend with your kids. Schedule time to work. Don't let life happen to you. Take control of your life. Buy a daily planner and plan out your days. I love using Sundays to plan out my week ahead. This helps me stay focused on what's ahead and puts my priorities right in front of my face so I can adjust them if needed.*

Goal of This Chapter: *The goal of this chapter is to give you practical tips to help you be successful in your life- personally, at home and at work. From planning, learning and speaking the truth over your life, you'll learn ways to become your best you! It will urge you to fearlessly dive into the life God has called you to live.*

Be Okay With Not Being Normal

"You realize you're not normal", my young friend said as I told her our plans for the weekend. We were spending the weekend together as a family, as usual, and we had a date night planned that evening, where she would be babysitting. "Yeah, I know. But it's goal planning night and we are so excited to talk about this year's goals for our family. We will swing by the bookstore before dinner and grab a few new ones too!" She looked at me like I was a weirdo. In that moment, I knew. We were not normal.

If you're a stay-at-home-mom who felt called to raise your babies, maybe even homeschool, and care for those under your roof, and you get complete fulfillment out of doing that, power to you, girlfriend. Seriously, I envy you some days. Somedays I wish I had a calling to homeschool my kids and I wish I were content to stay home with them and take care of them each day with a smile. But God put a different dream in my heart and He made my calling different than yours. Does that make me better or more capable than you? Absolutely not. He created us and gifted us all uniquely.

If you're a mom working a 9-5 job and coming home to care for your kids after a long day's work, hats off to you, sister. You're killing it! I know you sometimes feel berated for wanting to, or even needing to, work all those long hours. The truth is, if your heart is right with God and you're doing what you need to do for your family and to serve the Lord well, then keep on trucking! We all have skill sets that make us different and capable of different things!

I am in the weird dilemma dynamic where I don't stay home full-time and I don't work full-time. I don't even work from home full-time. There is no category for someone like me and that's okay. I make my own schedule but have always been very strict in knowing I need to work 2 days per week outside of the home. If that means Mother's-Day-Out Programs or hiring a sitter, that's what I do. Some weeks are more than this, I can add two more days to my week pretty easily, but it's never less than this. Even though I don't have a boss watching over my shoulder making sure I'm getting my hours in, that's not the point. I want to work and getting in my time matters to me. My success depends upon my effort. It's equally important for me to spend plenty of time with my kids each week. I have two days devoted to spending time with them. I also have to answer phone calls, check emails and text clients during these times, but they know this and understand it. It's part of what Mommy does and I'm showing my kids what it looks like to work hard and balance many things as a Mompreneur.

I've always been okay with not being normal. It's an important part of allowing God to use you in his way, for his purpose. You have to be okay with standing out and not quite fitting into society's standards.

Life lessons, y'all. They are not always easy or fun. They hurt and growth takes sacrifice. Here are some things I have learned as I have grown and I know you can relate!

1) To reach your calling, you cannot let someone else decide who you are meant to be.
2) There are always going to people rooting for you to fail. That's what makes you know you're doing something worthwhile.
3) It doesn't matter what people say about you or what you occasionally say to yourself. It only matters what God says about you!

Amen and Amen.

Success Leaves Clues

*"Success leaves clues. Study people you admire and
want to be like." - Tony Robbins*

I have learned that I want to study people who are two
steps ahead of me! I don't want to learn from those
who are doing what I'm doing. If I want to better
myself, I have to learn from those who are doing it
even better AND the RIGHT way. I'm not going to
follow those who are running their businesses in a
way that is not honorable, not decent and not
trustworthy. I don't want to be like them so why would
I study their business model? I will learn from those
who are great, stable and who exemplify who I want
to be. Even when they seem so far ahead of me that I
think I may never catch them. That's okay because
their plan may not be God's plan for me.

A big part of succeeding is planning your year ahead,
your months before they happen and your days
before they occur. I highly recommend getting
yourself a good planner and working in it daily to keep
your tasks straight, make sure you're doing the right
activities and tracking your goals.

I always have these things in my bag: my planner, my
sermon notes, writing journal and 2019 goals planner.

If you want to be successful, work on bettering
yourself professionally, personally and spiritually.

Keep your ego in check; stay humble and hustle hard.

SHOW YOUR PEOPLE YOU CARE

People don't care how much you know until they know how much you care. How are you showing your clients that you care? Do you have a plan in place to show people that you value them? The best way to do this is by being relatable. It doesn't have to be fancy. Handwritten notes go a long way to show someone you care. Birthday cards, anniversary cards or in my case, home anniversary cards are a special way to show your clients you remember them! I have also learned the value of holding an annual event to show clients you appreciate them. This is a not a necessity but it is a tool to help show your appreciation.

As you game plan your strategy for showing your clients that you care, think about those three questions. How can you show them that you are trustworthy? By being relatable. Be professional yet don't pretend that you know it all. Prove yourself. If you want to be trustworthy, then prove yourself trustworthy. The Bible says: If you are faithful in the little things, you will be faithful in the large ones. But if you are dishonest in the little things, you won't be honest with greater responsibilities. (Luke 16:10) So if you do the little things for people (such as answering your phone and returning texts, being polite and respectful, taking care of tasks in a timely manner, doing your job well), they will trust you to do even more for them.

Creating raving fans - As a business owner of a business that relies on referrals, our goal should be to create raving fans. That means, doing such a good job for someone during your time together that they want to tell their friends all about it!

"Whatever you do, do it well. Do it so well that when people see you do it, they will want to come back and see you do it again and they will want to bring others and show them how well you do what you do."
- Walt Disney

This is #goals. This is what referral-based business looks like. This is what it looks like to treat people right and get referrals if you're in the "people business". Any sales business is people business. The quicker you learn that, the quicker your career will take off! Go back to the basics and treat people well, get really good at what you do in your business, follow-up ALWAYS and be consistent. This is what it takes to succeed.

Enjoy the Season You're In

I often hear people say "I can't wait to get out of college" or "I can't wait to be a mom". Even things like "This day needs to hurry up" or "I can't wait until the weekend". We have to be careful about wishing life away and not taking advantage of the moment. The "precious present" is all we really have control over, as the past is gone and the future lies ahead out of our reach and control. We can only live in the moment we have right now! I always tell college students to really enjoy those years, live fully in them, embrace classes and friendships and late nights and silly fun. Those days hold some of my best memories and I'm so glad I fully embraced them and can look back and smile. I want to do that in these days I'm in right now! I want to look back on motherhood and say "those were good days. I'm so glad I lived them intentionally, enjoyed the moments and can smile when I remember". I want to look back at the days of working and leading my team, with the joyous days and the tough days, and I want to say "that was awesome. Even if it wasn't always full of easy days. It was full of days that mattered. I got to do what I loved and I helped a lot of people along the way!" This can be said with many areas of our life - marriage, motherhood, sisterhood, church life, work life, the Golden Years and beyond! Let's stop just looking forward to the next season and start living in the present one. As Trace Adkins says in his country song "It won't be like this for long". If you haven't heard it, grab a box of tissues, turn it on Spotify and get ready to be moved.

Get Out of the Barn!

We raise goats at our house. It's a lot of fun for our kids to see the baby goats born, to raise them, take care of them and then watch the seasons change as those babies become moms to new baby goats. It shows our kids the circle of life in a prominent way. And let's face it, baby goats are just the cutest! Whenever we have friends over, their kids' first question is "when can we go see the goats"? It's a fun time and great entertainment! As I observe the goats, I learn things and wonder why they do certain things and how sometimes, those things they do are exactly what we do, as humans.

When the nanny goat has her baby, or babies (they can have up to 4 at a time!), we place them in the warm barn filled with hay and lock the gate so they are forced to bond. The mother goats must stay still so the baby can nurse and the baby "kid" needs warmth and attention from its mother, especially during the first few days of life. On nice, warm days, we let the baby goats and mothers out to run around and enjoy the fresh air and sunshine! As I walk around the land, I glance at the goats and, by golly, if those stinkers aren't back in that barn, right where they started! They have a whole pasture in front of them, fresh hay to eat, room to run and explore. Instead, they go back into the confines of the barn, into that small space where they are yet again, trapped. Why do they do this, I wonder to myself. And then I realize, it's safe, warm and comfortable. They know nothing can get them in there, no harm can be found in that small area. Yes, it stinks, it's confined and it's cramped, but it's their comfort zone. When they could have room to flourish, they choose the barn.

Aren't we that way sometimes? God gives us a new life, he says "go and live your life to the fullest! Live out your purpose that I have called you for!" And we go back to the comfortable "barn", or in our case, the "safe life". For you, that may mean hiding in your house, or staying in that safe job (which you hate but are too afraid to leave), it may mean a bad relationship (with a friend who is negative and not good for your spirit). It may even mean being afraid to try a new church, take a new position at work, or start fresh with your kids. Friend, it's never too late to start a dream that God places in your heart and now is the time! If we will take the step into faith and get out of the comfy barn, fresh life awaits! New adventures, new people who need your influence, new life experiences and better friendships await. If we can get out of our comfort zones for just a little while, knowing that the first step is usually the hardest to take, we can step into our God-given gifts and potential. Once we do that, we can look back and see that our "barn" was just a smelly, confined mess. Yes, it was necessary for a while, but when life opens up, we must leave the comfort and step into the new horizon!

When the baby goats are about two months old, they are eating hay and grain well and not solely dependent on their Mommas, we let them both out into the field with the other goats. They are free! Are there predators that could try to attack them, either a hawk in the air or a coyote who finds a hole in the fence? Sadly, yes. Do they have to learn how to thrive outside the tiny barn and without their mother constantly at their side? Again, yes. Do they need room to grow, learn and stretch their little legs? Yes, yes, yes. And when they do, they stay out of that stinky barn and they just want to run free! You can do that too. Once you leave the comfort zone and take a step into your calling, the barn becomes a distant memory and you will know that you were made for so much more!

NO Fear Attitude - Risks are not risky when you don't fear the risk.

As Easy As Riding A Bike

We have two kids who are learning to ride their bikes. Our daughter wanted her training wheels off early and can easily ride her bike solo at six years old. Our son is currently going through the learning process and he gets easily frustrated when he can't pedal and keep up with those little legs, even with the training wheels attached. He tries, falls over and cries. Oh, the cries of a four-year-old. "I'll never be able to do this!" I hear him say these words and it's hard not to laugh at his little boy voice. I know this is not true because he has already come so far from that little trike he used to ride. I know that in a few months he will be flying down the road on his big boy bike, this current frustration only a distant setback. But right now, he is struggling. "My legs burn", "it's too windy", "I keep falling over". I listen and try to help, as we teach him how to sit up straight and ride his bike the correct way. I realize that even as adults, we can behave this way in life.

We want things now and we cannot see that God has already brought us so far from where we used to be. We used to use "training wheels" in life and we have stepped up to the next level, time and again. Yes, our legs burn, the wind may be too strong at times and maybe we keep falling over due to life's storms. But God knows that in order for us to take off those training wheels and move up again and again, we must endure these temporary trials. Burning legs make our legs stronger. Wind makes us learn to push through and keep going. Falling over teaches us to sit up straighter, adjust our helmet and ride confidently. As we grow, develop and get to the next levels of our lives, may we not complain and whine. For we know that pain is temporary. God sees our potential and his vision for us is eternal.

I'm learning that all successful people have top ingredients that are always present. I've come up with an acronym for this: GROW.

> *Grit*
> *Resilience*
> *Outlook*
> *Weird*

Let's go over these four ingredients and break down what they mean in detail.

Grit - There is no substitute for this one. Good things come to those who hustle. Grit is a combination of hustle and a "never quit" attitude. It's that "X-Factor" that you see in a successful person and wonder what makes them tick. Grit makes those who want it bad enough do everything they can to get it. Grit cannot simply be given, it must be desired and sought after. It's something that's planted deep. When someone has it, you just know it.

Resilience - John Maxwell says that everything worthwhile is uphill- building a business, raising a family. Resilience is what keeps up going when the going gets tough. It's the mindset that there is no back-up plan or Plan B. Resilient people succeed because they don't know there is another option.

Outlook - Successful people always have an outlook that is bigger than the here and now. They are fearlessly optimistic and see the big picture when thinking about their lives. They have BIG WHYS and they have dreams that are scary and even crazy.

Weird - This one sounds funny, I know. But most successful people I know are not "normal" in the way society views them. They do things differently, they chose a different lifestyle, they live in a different way with their families and they run their businesses in a way that not many can understand. In order to be successful, you must be okay with not being normal, and in fact, you must learn to embrace it.

Start Before You're Ready

If I had to give you the best piece of advice for propelling yourself forward, it would be this: Start before you're ready. Don't wait for the perfect time. There will never be a perfect time. Don't wait until your kids are older. Don't wait until you know more, achieve more or are more secure. Just as you're never ready to have baby, you'll never be ready to start a business or grow a business or have another baby. Nothing can prepare you for what it's really like. You must step out of the unknown and into the scary place of feeling like you may fall. You may just find that, without a safety net, you will fly.

SHINE
by Ashley

Instead of deleting, how about you choose to be the one who shines the light?

In a world full of darkness and negativity, don't hide out. Stand out.

Deleting is easy. Defeating is golden.

Discussion Questions:

Do you have GRIT?

_____

_____

_____

_____

What area of GRIT can you work on?

_____

_____

_____

_____

How can you move fearlessly forward?

_____

_____

_____

_____

Conclusion

Here is what I have to tell you- the road you have chosen will not be easy. The path you have chosen will be full of bumps, trials and bruises. You'll learn and grow, and then you will get knocked down and question everything. You'll pray a lot and you'll wonder why God put this dream in your heart. Your kids will wear you down and you'll feel weary and unqualified on some days. You'll strike out on some things in your business. You'll need to re-build and work through some messes. You'll work until midnight and push past the point of tired. You'll cry and you'll doubt your abilities. Your kids will scream and fuss and fight. You'll realize that you were born for a greater purpose and you'll feel God calling you forward. You'll say yes. You'll pick yourself back up and be thankful that God chose you to fulfill this particular calling. You'll rally and you'll succeed. You'll stand on podiums and realize that it was all worth it. You'll touch lives and make a difference. Your children will grow and they will flourish. You'll realize that it was worth it and everything you went through, everything you thought and everything that happened was for a purpose. You'll discover that you have raised a business and your babies. You'll thank the Lord that He chose you.

I pray that God uses this book to reach you, teach you and bless you. I pray that the words between these pages have filled you with a sense of purpose as you move forward into the life God is calling you toward! I pray that you'll never be afraid of failing and that whenever in doubt, you'll "do it afraid". ~ Ashley

Acknowledgements

To Bronson: Thank you, babe, for always believing in my ideas and never telling me I'm crazy. For every wild idea I've thrown at you, you have always encouraged me. Thank you for allowing me to rearrange our living room and plan our weekends with a smile. You are the perfect man for me. I love you and I love our life together. I can't wait to see our next years of crazy endeavors together.

To Brylee: You are so smart, sweet and thoughtful. You're a natural-born leader. Whatever you do in life, I know you will be great. You tackle everything with determination and the desire to be excellent. I look forward to our years ahead as we have mother/daughter days, family trips and weekday walks and games because I just love being with you. Mommy loves you!

To Bowen: Your kind heart and sweet spirit is captivating. You keep our life interesting and fun. I cannot imagine our life without you in it because you bring us so much laughter and joy. You and I have a special bond and it will only grow over the years. I love you so much.

To Baker: You are connected to Mommy, always wanting to be by my side. You are happy to play with others or content being alone. It's so fun to watch your personality come out as you grow and develop. Your smile is the best thing in the world. You are becoming a big boy and I'm blessed to me your Mommy. I love you.

To Benaiah: You are my little angel and this first year with you has been nothing short of amazing. You are the sweetest, happiest baby boy and God made you perfectly ours. You will always be my little lion chaser. We prayed for you and love you so much.

To my Mom and Dad: Thanks for raising me to work hard and value family and my relationship with Jesus first. Your love always made me feel safe, sure and confident. I love you.

To Pastor Josh: Thank you for your thoughtful sermons which always create inspiration in me. The church has helped show me where my true calling lies and how I can be bold where God has placed me. I am thankful for your vision and leadership.

About the Author

Ashley Schubert is a wife and mother of four children. Through having four babies in five years and starting a new business, she quickly learned how to find a balance and not let excuses stand in her way. She is a top-producing Real Estate Agent in Oklahoma where she has sold over $50 Million in the residential market in six years. She leads Flourish Real Estate Group and has won the honors of OKC Rising Star, President's Circle Gold and is a top 2% Realtor nationwide. She is a Christian Women's Author and Speaker and is passionate about inspiring women to reach their full potential in their businesses and at home with their families. She hosts a podcast called Y'all Are Crazy and interviews guests about balancing their families and businesses while keeping God at the center of it all. She and her family reside in Edmond, Oklahoma where they enjoy spending time outdoors and taking care of their goats.

Instagram: AshleySchubert_speaks
www.yallarecrazy.com

Made in the USA
Monee, IL
17 July 2020